WHY I KNOW
THERE IS A GOD

OTHER BOOKS BY FULTON OURSLER

FULTON OURSLER

WHY
I KNOW
THERE
IS
A GOD

DOUBLEDAY & COMPANY, INC.

GARDEN CITY, NEW YORK, 1951

CONTENTS

INTRODUCTION

*I*N OFFERING this small volume to the public my intention is to help those who are seeking truth, by telling personal experiences of myself, and of others, of far greater usefulness in the world, who know God and love Him and serve Him.

One can know there is a God most completely by loving God and serving Him, and so I have presented here examples of what happens when one dedicates a life to His service. I see truth dramatically, expressed in the way men and women act and react in this mysterious world. So, having said, as simply as I know how, why I know there is a God, I have gone on to tell what that knowledge can mean in human experience—largely with the hope and, truthfully, the prayer that others will try the experiment for themselves.

To believe before you know does sound like a contradiction of logic, and yet "the soul's invincible surmise" has led many a Columbus to many a new world. And logic

7

would have kept him at home, comfortably at ease in his errors.

Here, at least, is the brief story of one man who had no faith in faith itself—and how he found it. Here are stories of what other men have done, once they were possessed by faith. Here is an invitation for every unbeliever to take a really experimental attitude and seek God for himself.

And may the dear God bless us all.

FULTON OURSLER

WHY I KNOW
THERE IS A GOD

To April
with Love

1

WHY I KNOW THERE IS A GOD

*M*Y SEARCH began more than fifty years ago. One morning in April my colored nurse led me to the door of a gray-stone chapel at Twenty-third Street and Guilford Avenue, in Baltimore. Welcoming me inside, a Sunday-school teacher awesomely informed me that I was now in God's house.

"Whereabouts," I asked, "is God?"

"God," the lady assured me, "is everywhere."

But I wanted Him to be somewhere. Like the little girl in the fable, I did not want Him to be invisible; I wanted Him "with skin on." That was why I refused to sit still on my little oaken chair, but ran about the room during the singing of "Little Drops of Water." I peeked under the pew and in a broom closet, only to be rescued finally, breathless and dusty, from behind the pipe organ, weeping because I had not found God.

Thus my quest began, and through half a century I never entirely abandoned it. Even in childhood the reality or non-reality of the Creator seemed to me the most important matter in life; nor can I understand today how any intelligent person can think otherwise. It is the one supreme matter on which a man has to be sure, for every decision he makes hinges upon it.

But can anyone really know? Lanland said: "I have swept the heavens with my telescope and have not found God." While other scientists testify: "We have examined the brain with our microscopes and have not found the soul!"

Yet I begin every day by speaking the words of the ancient creed:

"I believe in God, the Father Almighty, Maker of Heaven and Earth . . ."

I recite it all because I believe it all, even though some of my nearest and most intelligent friends challenge my belief.

"We know that you believe, all right," they say. "But you can't really know, now can you?"

"I do know," I assure them, and sometimes quote the Old Testament direction: "Be still, and know that I am God." However, in such friendly discussions it is much easier to know God than it is to keep still; that is the time when arguments begin.

And yet, a man has got to feel that he knows. A creed, a belief, can be of no lasting value if it does not prove itself. The great St. Paul tells us that those are blessed who believe although they have not seen. The blind man of Galilee believed first; not until then were his eyes opened and he saw men as trees walking. Faith comes first; but make no mistake about it, the man of faith does not linger in credulity; it is by his faith that he is led into the full light of knowledge. That is the divine paradox; we come to know when we believe, and not before.

Only those who have never known God will call this

transcendental experience an illusion. It is not wishful thinking; it is a sublime reality. But it is difficult to convey to others. The man who tries to confide the experience of hearing Beethoven's Fifth Symphony to a deaf man has a much easier task. Still, the deaf man's misfortune does not make the music an illusion; it is, instead, a vivid fact and a blessing upon the man whose ears and soul are open to its beauty. Now arises a magnificent difference: not everyone can hear an orchestra, but everyone can hear the voice of the Father. The supreme franchise of the human soul is that it can know God. The supreme tragedy of today's tormented world is that so many do not know Him.

When I say such things to some of my friends, who are earnest doubters, they demand to know how anyone can ever prove that God exists. To that question there are two answers, two keys to the most exciting mystery of life.

The first way to know God is by sheer reason, through the brain. That was my first way. Surely, I told myself, if logic is a science, then one should be able to prove or disprove the existence of God scientifically. I knew that physicists had often established beyond dispute the reality of things which could neither be seen nor heard, nor ever known by other senses. Has any eye ever seen an atom? Yet the survivors of Hiroshima and Nagasaki know its terrible actuality. Again, all the billions upon billions of genes in the world could be contained in one child's thimble. Beyond vision or touch, these particles have, nevertheless, been demonstrated; they exist, reservoirs of incredible power.

Every high school student knows how, once upon a time, an astronomer discovered a star without ever having looked upon it. So exact was his knowledge of stellar mathematics

that he calculated—he did not have to believe; he *knew*—
that there must be another planet in our solar system or else
the whole celestial circus would fly apart. Later on, when
larger telescopes were built, astronomers could actually see
that planet. But it had already been discovered by sheer
reason. So, through the same mechanism of the intellect,
our Father in Heaven also clearly reveals Himself to the
logical mind. You don't have to read the profundities of
St. Thomas Aquinas to find this for yourself. These read-
able books will give you the scientific, intellectual proofs
of God: *The Truths Men Live By*, by John A. O'Brien
(Macmillan); *Man Does Not Stand Alone*, by A. Cressy
Morrison (Revell); and *Human Destiny*, by Pierre Le-
comte du Nöuy (Longmans).

But many another person like myself recoils from skull-
busting theological complexities. I preferred firsthand
knowledge. While it was possible, I told myself, for a man
to read a textbook on swimming and come to know aquatics
thoroughly, solely by diagrams and theory, I would rather
plunge in a pool and swim. We all exult in the joy of experience, free motion, the splendor of survival in another
element.

That is the second way to know God—by personal experience. That was my second way.

In my search for truth I had already explored many
different fields. A study of comparative religions over a
decade of years led me from Buddhism, and its Western
translation called Theosophy, all the way to Bahaism and
Zoroastrianism, with many stops between. As a reporter for
the *Baltimore American*, I had also attended many religious conferences, and for three months I covered evange-
listic meetings of Billy Sunday. I had been immersed in

doctrine. I had even waited for specters in dark-room séances of spiritualist mediums. Out of all this I emerged, at the age of thirty, a self-styled agnostic. In those days I considered myself a liberal person, emancipated from superstition, although still genially loyal to ethical values —when they did not interfere too much with what I wanted to do.

I declared that I believed in live and let live. Circumstances, I felt, altered not some cases, but all. There were no absolutes. No more right or wrong. And—for me—no more authority, and no more revelation. Certainly no more supernaturalism. All these things were anathema to my emancipated and rational mind. I couldn't be like Christ, I told myself; I would just be myself.

Such tolerance and emancipation and what I considered common sense and good will should have brought me happiness but did not. Nor did they bring happiness to anyone I knew. Most of my friends felt as I did; none of us better or worse than the other, I suppose; all very independent and self-reliant and disdainful of the old-fashioned faith of our fathers. We all had a great deal of fun, too, but somehow our hilarities left us dispirited. No part of life was ever really satisfying. With our freedom *and* our liberal principles we should have known a high sense of spiritual well-being, of contented integrity. But was it true freedom? It was certainly not true liberalism. Not one of us knew any real security. Instead, we all had an inner restlessness of disappointment and discontent. Nothing was ever as sweet to see, hear, taste, touch, or feel as we, in our expectations, hoped it would be. At every pay-off we were always let down—and, one way or another, there was always a hangover.

This inner sulkiness and depression had nothing to do with material success. Among my friends were many who had achieved fame and riches, or, at least, a lot of money in the bank. But no matter how much more wealth they piled up, how often their pictures were on the front page, their new possessions, their new wives—nothing was ever enough. After they got what they wanted, they didn't want it. Without avail, they haunted doctors and psychiatrists and yogis.

The world in which I lived was a world of self-pity, self-justification, alibis, envies, jealousies, greeds, fears, resentments, grudges, and hatreds. Today was never good enough, but tomorrow they hoped to be glad. I say they, but I mean we. Today there are eight million men and women quite like us, who are under mental care. There will be, psychiatrists tell us, ten million more in a year or so. People who find the burden of life too much for them; their brain rebels and seeks escape in fantasy.

I shall be forever grateful that in the midst of mental bleakness I found the way out. It is not easy to tell how this happened; I cannot bring myself to open old wounds to public gaze. But you may remember the true story of the illustrious refugee at Lourdes, a famous liberal writer who, with his wife, had slipped through the Nazi frontier. They were working their way southward from Germany through France. The Gestapo was after them, and capture meant the concentration camp or worse. Their hope was to cross the Spanish border and sail for the United States. But they were stopped by Spanish officials. Bribes and entreaty alike failed; they were turned back and found a lodging in the little town in the Pyrenees called Lourdes. On his first night there the fugitive writer stood in front of the famous shrine and made a prayer, a cry from the heart.

"I do not believe in you," he said, in effect, "and I must be honest and say so. But my danger is great, and in my extremity, on the chance that you might after all be real, I ask your help. See my wife and me safely across the barrier, and when I get to the United States I will write the story of this place for all the world to read."

Having finished his prayer, he returned to his hotel. Never, he told me later, had he known a calm so deep; it was pure peace reaching him from beyond; he had touched something beyond the prison of the five senses.

Strange as it sounds, Franz Werfel and his wife got safely through, within the week. The first thing he did, once safe in our land, was to write *The Song of Bernadette*. In our day no more popular tribute to faith was ever penned than the story written by the refugee novelist. Before he died he told me that in the terror of his plight he had come to know God and thereafter had never lost the sense of His presence.

Now something akin to that happened to me. It was nothing so spectacular as a flight from Hitler's agents, but within my own modest sphere I, too, felt surrounded and in danger and afraid. My agnostic self-reliance was no longer helpful; trouble came and littered on my doorstep. Not only I but those nearest and dearest to me were in trouble with me, until I felt I really needed God's help. Yet even then I could not, as an intelligent man, command myself to believe, or pretend to obey—for a man is a fool who tries to deceive either God or himself. The most—the best that I could manage was to admit to myself that I wished I could believe.

And that was enough!

Faith is a gift—but you can ask for it! "O Lord," prayed a man in the Bible, "I believe; help Thou mine unbelief." As he laid his situation before God, and as Werfel did, so did I. Not in Palestine, nor in the Pyrenees, but close to the fashionable parade on Fifth Avenue. On a blustery day, with dark clouds lowering, I turned suddenly into a house of God and asked for the gift of faith. And in the chapel, I took one more vital step.

"In ten minutes or less I may change my mind," I prayed. "I may scoff at all this—and love error again. Pay no attention to me then. For this little time I am in my right mind and heart. This is my best. Take it and forget the rest; and, if You are really there, help me."

It was a striking omen to me that when I came out on the steps the sun had crashed through the dark skies and the lordly avenue was full of color and light. There was a curious feeling of hope in my heart; not peace, but the confident expectancy of peace.

Merely for the record, and not to prove anything whatever, let me say that as Werfel was brought safely to the United States, so the perplexities of my problem were most remarkably and swiftly disposed of. Only chance would explain it to the unbelieving, because no human agency contrived the events. The complication dissolved itself by the oncoming of a series of what the rationalist would call beautiful coincidences. In two weeks I no longer had a serious problem.

In that result, of course, I was most fortunate. It might easily have been otherwise. Yet do not mistake me. Even so, as I know now, my petition would have been heard. Millions of prayers go up every instant, and every one is answered—but sometimes the answer is no.

The old Greeks had a saying that when the gods were angry with a man they answered his prayers. A little boy implores his father for a bicycle. There is nothing inherently wrong with such a request. But if the neighborhood is dangerous because of traffic, the wise father has to refuse. It is hard for the child to grasp that wisdom. In perfect trust one learns to say, "Thy will be done," knowing that whatever answer comes, is best.

But for me the real knowing of God was just beginning on that day. Only incidentally is prayer asking for help. One should have to ask favors of God no oftener than a sensible child asks favors of his father on earth. Prayer is not a slot machine, where you drop in a request and a boon comes tumbling out of the bottom. We do pray for help, but oftener we pray for help for others, and even oftener we pray our thanks for blessings already received. Above everything else, we pray daily in sheer felicity, in communion, in close contact with the Father, asking nothing whatever but the joy of knowing Him.

It is through prayer that we know there is a God, that God is there; through prayer that we know *Him*—as Father and friend.

Now here the skeptics turn away in disdain. I can never figure out why. If they admit that they have never known God, and I maintain that I have known and do continue to know Him, and that the path to that knowing is through prayer, then why, in the name of God, do they not pray, just to test it? Why don't they find out by personal experience?

The materialist will deride prayer as a superstitious practice, a psychological hoax, a self-hypnosis, an illogical conception, a childish folly—but never will he put his prejudice to the test in his own discontented life. Tell him that prayer is the only way to God, and he will reject that way. "Bring Him on, face to face," he demands. "Nothing else will do for me."

He wants to rewrite the universal law to meet his own requirements. He is like a man from Mars who is suspicious of photography, sure that it is some kind of trick. "Why," he demands, "do you have to go into that darkroom and do things? That's where the trick is. Let's see you develop and print a picture right out here in the broad light of day. That can't be done, now can it?"

No, you have to have darkness to find a picture on the sensitive plate, and you have to have prayer to bring out the invisible presence of God.

But once a man can lift from his soul old Adam's curse of pride, once he finds the humility to ask himself: "Where was I when Thou laidst the foundations of the world?"—once he can, with the perfect trust of a child, reach out to the invisible Father—then comes grace abounding, and a man knows God most intimately; nearer than breathing, closer than the hands and feet.

God meant it, too, when He said in the first commandment that He was jealous and would have no others before Him. He wants you—all of you. You have opened the door; He will come in and take possession. And at once you find yourself plagued with a vague unease that comes equally with His peace. Your daily life becomes a whole series of paradoxes like that.

Possessed of a new feeling of profound tranquillity, nevertheless, you want to be active. Your kind instincts will no longer be satisfied with sending checks to worthy charities; you will be ashamed to buy yourself off. That is

like the old Civil War custom whereby a draftee, if he had
the money, could hire a substitute to do his fighting for
him. It is hiring others to serve God for you. Such gifts to
charity are necessary, but never enough. We have to do
the corporal works of mercy ourselves; and, as we come to
know God, the urge to serve Him personally becomes overpowering. We must feed the hungry, visit the sick, comfort the widow and orphan, clothe the naked, shelter the
shelterless—under our own roof, with our own bare hands.

That is when a human being comes closest to God and
knows Him best.

Isn't it strange that it should have taken me fifty years to
find that simple key to the mystery? Ten thousand times in
ten thousand days of that half century, God walked with me
to school, rode with me in the bus, held out a beggar's hand
at the corner alley, roared at me in the very blasphemy of a
reeling old sot from whom all had fled. So many times He
was at my elbow, and I pushed on, unaware. Fifty years of
never noticing! I have much lost time to make up for.

The skeptic deserves to be assured that all that faith will
bring a man can also be justified by his intellect. But that
process, I dare to think, can wait. If a man would find God,
let him humbly ask for a chance to believe; and, meanwhile, let him go personally and not by delegate to his less
fortunate brothers—and sisters—helping the needy of body
and soul. He will presently find what he seeks. For when
a man can leave himself and enter the lives of others, he
leaves his own heart open so that God may enter and dwell
with him. This blessing I wish on every reader of these
lines.

2

RETURN TO REALITY

I REGARD the change in my thinking during the last ten years as a rediscovery of truth, best described by the unpopular, old-fashioned word conversion. A man's principal business on the earth, I have come to realize, is to know God, to love Him and serve Him. And by Him I refer to the Father, Son, and Holy Ghost.

This process of conversion has not turned my world upside down, although at times it has seemed to do so. It has, instead, set me on my feet again, whereas for nearly half a century I was trying to think things out while standing on my head.

In my former topsy-turvy state I rejected the authority of Church and scripture, as claims based on readily demonstrable fallacies.

There was, as I have said, no absolute whatever: no right, no wrong. Everything depended on conditioning, on heredity and environment and chance, on biological and economic determinism. The old notion of the existence of good and evil, warring forces of light and darkness, was an exploded myth. Had I not read Haeckel, Freud, Schopenhauer, White, Dewey, and Frazer's *Golden Bough?*

As for God, if He existed at all, He was some impersonal, unknowable force, and nothing could be more absurd than to conceive Him in anthropomorphic terms. Certainly there was no Father in Heaven to whom one could pray.

Education was the one true hope for the world, and nothing must be allowed to stand in the way of its objectivity. With increasing knowledge, who could take the Ten Commandments seriously? Any God who was a jealous God would just have to get over his jealousy. Take the ban against giving false witness. I believed in truth—or thought I did; but, like many of my fellows, when necessary I used a lie to advance my purposes, every one of which I considered worthy. Thus I acted on the principle that the end justified the means. Today the lie, as a weapon —an instrument—is the grisly symbol of a widespread school of thought of which I was once a pupil. And often, when accused, I took refuge in the arms of Pilate, defying critics to define truth, a dodge as shoddy today as in the procurator's time.

To be told not to kill, and to ignore the widespread suffering of helpless sick people, was an outrage; rebelling against that commandment, too, I endorsed euthanasia. Adultery was practiced so widely that to condemn it seemed a futile and silly gesture. Someday a poll of sex habits would be taken, and we would all see how universal sexual liberation was in fact, if not in theory. Eventually such a poll was taken by one scientist, although first essayed by another who frankly declared that Christianity must give way to the enjoyment of intercourse as it was known in pagan societies. While I winced at that proposal, I also thought I must not, under any circumstances, be a prude.

As for coveting other men's wives, a form of successive

polygamy was habitually practiced by Americans who could afford it, and that seemed to me often a sensible arrangement. All other familiar repudiations of the Ten Commandments I also approved.

Clearly, I thought, the problems of mankind were to be solved without supernatural interference. The right way to proceed was to analyze each problem, plan the solution, organize to carry out the plan, supervise the organization —and there you were! Or should be! The brain of man would prove itself equal to any task. I was proud of man.

Thus the importance of religion remained wholly in the social gospel, by which specialists might implement plans to improve the lot of the less fortunate; a mechanization, an industrialization of good works. In this sort of effort I foresaw that political action would become inevitable.

Possibly the clearest way to successful political action lay through Socialism, although of this I was not quite sure. At any rate, I saw no basic conflict between Marxism and the humanitarian goal. Christian Socialism did not appear to me as an irreconcilable contradiction. There might even be such a thing as Christian Communism. Under a different political system the welfare of the people would be lifted to undreamed-of heights. At this point I began to think of myself as a sensibly virtuous man, full of vision and practical love of my fellows. Build enough playgrounds, schools, good houses, and hospitals; establish a health program to reach everyone, and earth would become the kingdom of Heaven.

As for the world, the way to peace lay through an association of governments, but one with no taint of religion. To that great enterprise there must be no religious note, for two reasons: (a) the people of the world worshiped differently; (b) Russia didn't care for any worship whatever, and it would be wiser to leave out God rather than Russia.

Irony aside, my thinking exalted the unassisted cerebration of man. He could, in my view, plan himself into felicity.

All supernaturalism was anathema. The virgin birth, the divinity of Christ, the miracles were sheer superstition, with counterparts in various marvel religions. While accepting some of the teachings of Christianity, I disagreed with others; holding further that many matters most important to human behavior it had shockingly ignored. I regarded organized religion as a failure, often a pious fraud.

Not one of these thoughts do I think today. Instead, I have come to know them to be a mass of glittering rubbish, castoff tinsel from a carnival of wishful thinking. I have rehearsed the history of how the change was wrought in me. That was an intimate experience; first a metamorphosis of spirit, and of mind afterward. But faith was buttressed with much study.

The result, as I regard it, was a return to reality.

Suppose—as many imaginative writers have liked to suppose—that an intelligent citizen of some other planet should land on this globe. With no previous knowledge, this visitor would be immediately confounded by what he saw. With the ruins of two wars staring him in the face, he would wonder why on earth we were getting ready for a third one. Beholding whole peoples dying from hunger, and other whole peoples enchained in slavery; and finding all nations beset by hatreds, suspicions, and world-wide dread, he would have to ask himself: "Why do these mortals gravitate to the selfish rather than the unselfish? Why are they naturally cruel instead of kind?"

And he would then have to conclude that somewhere along the line some terrible tragedy had overtaken the human race.

At that precise point he would be back in the midst of the first chapters of Genesis. Back to the fall of man; to original sin, from which primal handicap no one of us is exempt. From there it would be a natural step to the four Gospels and man's redemption through Christ, Our Lord.

So first, like Nicodemus, I learned that a man must be born again before he is fit to plan a Heaven on earth for his brothers. My first return was to the undisturbed reality of the Holy Bible; to its authority and inspiration and truth through revelation. Too long I had been bespelled by the false glitter of a scholarship of guesswork as deficient in humility as opinion polls—and about as accurate. Now that I was about it, I discovered that "scientific" criticism of the Scriptures was far more vulnerable than the texts it accused.

Against the ponderous chatter of experts I saw that I had to accept Christ as one of three things—as God, madman, or charlatan. There was no other choice; logic could not sustain the theory that He was simply a good man. Nor could logic maintain against His record either insanity or insincerity. There was left only the fact that He must be what He said He was.

This was enough to set me firmly on my feet.

I had thought my finite mind could understand the infinite; what Poe had called the "mad pride of intellectuality" had made me presumptuously forget my proper place; unless I became as a little child, as Jesus had plainly stated, I did not have a chance to find truth. Nor did anyone else in the world. Honest thinking cannot even begin without humility.

But when one does seek to think as a child of God, all petty doubts of the infinite powers of God pass off quickly, like the pains of a fever. In their place comes an eagerness to know Him better, an increase of love for Him, and a great desire to serve. In place of self-pity, of excuses because of conditioning, environment and heredity, one becomes aware of the great gift of free will, the power of choice, the search for understanding of how best we can serve.

Here the social gospel takes on a new meaning. It is not enough to serve on the board of an organization with plans to improve the condition of the less fortunate; not enough merely to write checks for worthy causes. The corporal and spiritual works of mercy are a personal obligation for me to do myself as well as by organization. Otherwise the letter will kill the spirit. I saw that the social gospel, followed to the decline in personal service and personal piety, had promoted God upstairs to an honorary job with no authority, a familiar device in organizational technique when a new crowd takes over. But God is never mocked.

I must do His will as best I could grasp it with unremitting prayer, that cosmic force, intimate though vast, which, like the sun, warms me as with the Father's personal caress, and yet ripens the grain and raises the water to the clouds.

The spiritual life must be the goal of every thinking person. Only when the heart is right can the soul make decent use of its chief instrument, which is the brain. The world and I had foolishly thought the brain was all, and education its task. So Germany became the best-educated nation, and its thinking without God's help gave us Hitler.

Here it also became clear why this good Father was

jealous in His first commandment. Since he was the one true God, any other *must* be false—and one had to look, not only to Germany, where brute force and cunning were worshiped, and to Italy and Russia, but all around us at home, where the worship of intellectuality, materialism, and appetites was eating away at faith and decency.

There was not in that good, jealous Father's service any room for the lie. He had explicitly told us that we must know the truth, and the truth would make us free. That truth, too big for the petty mind of man, was not too big for his soul.

This soul might not grasp the details of all His laws, but it could know their righteousness; know that the universe was a friendly place, just and full of His mercy, even when disaster overwhelmed and one groaned and cried: "Why should this happen to me?"

Education of the mind and muscles was not enough. We had taught our young to know what they did not know; we must go on and teach them to behave as they had not behaved. The complete textbook for that behavior was the Holy Bible, all criticism notwithstanding. Professor Ernest M. Ligon, greatest of modern child experimenters, had given four years of his scientific life to the Yale Theological Seminary, only to declare, when he received his theological degree, that Jesus Christ was the soundest psychologist ever to guide mortal behavior.

In the commandments, and in His teachings, was the pattern of life. Euthanasia? It cannot be right, because it is a violation of revealed truth. No one will deny that the practice of slaying a suffering patient puts an end to his pain. But no one who has the slightest knowledge of human nature will believe that any safeguards can prevent the remedy from doing infinitely more harm than the troubles it cures.

I had a friend in the hospital and he was getting well. The doctors told me he could hope for ten more years of life in painless invalidism. Yet his wife pleaded with them to destroy the man; she said she could not bear to see her dear husband helpless. One suspects she really revolted at the idea of making good on her promise at the altar to take care of him in sickness as in health.

We are not worthy to tamper with the commandments. And the temptation to individuals is the least of the evils of euthanasia. Its grossest danger lies in the tyranny of governments. The preservation of the inviolability of human life is an essential to a free society. In my confused thinking I had seen only the benefits; the horror of the dangers is still not apparent to some of the most decent, yet muddled, people I know.

And so, too, with divorce. Of course those who are unhappily married enjoy life more when their obligations are removed. Any man would like to tear up any kind of contract when its clauses begin to run counter to his interest. That is why nations break treaties and make wars, and why we hang the perpetrators as criminals if one side wins. The sanctity of contracts is an essential to free society; when that sanctity is broken, we have juvenile delinquency and adult crime in such proportions that now we don't know what to do.

Man, with his brains, was denying the truths of revealed religion, relying on his own ideas, and making a mess of the world.

Yet many men of good will were fired with persistent zeal for these earthy notions of the brain. They ran after

Communism, some even calling it Christianity made practical. But in my new thinking I saw that Communism was not one thing, but two. It was, first, a philosophy which I rejected with all my soul; a philosophy that was a negation of Almighty God; a plan for man grounded on the nothingness of the individual, on the organization of ruthless power and the galvanic force of hate. The necessities of life were all it offered, not knowing that man does not live by bread alone. But Communism was also something more than a bitterly false philosophy. It was a criticism of the world as Christians had allowed the world to become. If the followers of Christ had truly followed the Master, that criticism could never have been made. The work of repair will have to begin now, but the answer lies, not in Marx and his *Manifesto*, but in the marks of the nails in His hands.

And how was I to live in a world with so many Communists? I must love them. Their unholy credo is a temporary thing; in a year or a thousand years it will be gone. But a Communist is immortal; he is potentially a child of God, sharing eternity with me. He is my brother and I may not hate him; I must help him if I can.

It is hard to be a Christian. But every criticism, true or not, should strengthen us; even if, as generally happens, the critic sees the mote in our eye, forgetting the beam in his own; though he judges others, forgetting that he himself may be judged. Peace to him, even so. He is doing us a service if he teaches us to pray harder, to seek to live more valiantly, to follow more determinedly in the footsteps of our Divine Master.

For what the world needs first is Christians—full of love, full of faith. Dark as seem these foolish years, He will lead us into the light.

3

OUR SECOND JOB

*S*OMETIMES people say:

"I would like to do some good in the world. But, with responsibilities at home, my nose is always to the grindstone. I am sunk in my own petty affairs, and there is no chance for my life to mean anything."

This is a common and dangerous error. To know the happiness of positive achievement, one does not have to neglect duties or do spectacular things. In helpfulness to others, every man can find, on his own doorstep, the adventures of the soul.

And while such experiences are secondary to a daily job, they are our surest source of true peace and lifelong satisfaction.

This was the theme of a breakfast conversation I was privileged to have with that great and supremely happy man, Albert Schweitzer. It was on one of his rare sabbaticals from his outpost in the equatorial inferno of West Africa that we broke bread together, one steamy summer morning, in the dining room of the Gramercy Park Hotel, in New York. There, over a cup of coffee, I first heard his doctrine of "the second employment."

Across the table from me sat a man who had given his health, his money, his every breath to the service of his God. A concert organist, a world-renowned Biblical scholar, a writer and philosopher, he had at the age of thirty given up these varied careers and entered medical school, thence to bury himself in the disease-cursed jungles of the Congo. In the more than thirty years that had passed since he and his wife first opened their hospital in an abandoned chicken coop at Lambaréné, their whole lives had been dedicated to the care of pygmies and cannibals. What more could a man offer God than that?

From the sun-baked lips of this man I first heard of "the second job"—a career for the spirit.

You have, he said, your everyday work—whether in a factory in Detroit, or a chicken coop in Africa—work that you must do first and do well; but close behind, treading on its heels, comes your No. 2 job, for which there is no pay except the privilege of doing it. But in the second job one encounters noble chances and finds deep strength; here all a man's reserve power can be put to work, for what the world lacks most today is men who occupy themselves with the needs of other men. In this unselfish labor a blessing falls on both the helper and the helped.

Without such spiritual adventures, said Schweitzer, the man of today walks in darkness. He loses himself in an atmosphere of inhumanity. The terrible truth is that, with the progress of history and the economic development of the world, it is becoming not easier but harder to produce true civilization. So, in modern society, a workman on the assembly line seems no longer an individual, becoming instead a part of a machine. What is his remedy?

He cannot rescue his manhood merely by seeking escape

in alcohol, shows, or gambling. In spite of mechanical daily work he can, however, assert his human personality in seizing every opportunity for spiritual activity. How? By his second employment; by means of personal action, however unpretending, for the good of his fellow men. He will not have to look far for opportunities.

Our greatest mistake, as individuals, is that we walk through our life with closed eyes, like blind people, and do not notice our chances. As soon as we open our eyes and deliberately search, we see many who need help, not in big things but in the littlest things. Wherever a man turns, he can find someone who needs him.

One day, Schweitzer told me, he was traveling through Germany in a third-class railway carriage. With him in the compartment rode a youth, who sat with folded hands and turned his head about, as if looking for something unseen. Facing him was a fretful old man, whose harassed eyes were never still. Presently the lad remarked that it would be dark before they reached the nearest large city.

"I don't know what I shall do when we get there," returned the old gentleman. "My son is in the hospital, very ill; my only one. I had a telegram to come at once. I want to see my son before he dies. But I am from the country; I don't know my way around the town. I hope I shall not get lost."

To which the young man replied:

"I know the city well. I will get off with you and take you straight to your son. Then I will take a later train."

As they left the compartment they walked together like brothers. Who can assay the effect of a small kind deed in a frightened world? One needs no more potent opportunity than to watch for the littlest things that need to be done.

During World War I, a cockney cab driver was declared too old for military service. He went from one bureau to another, offering to make himself useful in his spare time and always being turned away. Finally he gave himself his own commission. Soldiers from out-of-town camps were being allowed leave in the city before going to the front. So at eight o'clock the old cabby appeared at a railroad station and looked for puzzled troopers. Four or five times every night he served as guide through the maze of London streets, leading the strangers wherever they wanted to go and by the most direct route. His "second employment" was a success right up to demobilization.

We hesitate to approach a stranger from a feeling of embarrassment. The fear of being repulsed is the cause of a great deal of coldness in the world; when we seem indifferent we are often merely timid. The adventurous soul must break that barrier, resolving in advance not to mind a rebuff. If we dare with wisdom, always maintaining a certain reserve in our approach, we find that when we open ourselves, we open doors in others.

More than in the jungles of Africa, said the missioner of Lambaréné, the doors of the heart need to be opened in great cities. Love is always lonely in crowds. Country and village people know each other, and realize some common dependence, but the inhabitants of cities are strangers, who pass without salute—so isolated, so separate, lost and despairing. What a stupendous opportunity is waiting there for men and women who are willing to be simply human!

Begin anywhere—in office, factory, subway. There have been smiles across a streetcar aisle that may have stayed the purpose of a suicide. Each friendly glance or sign or hail is like a single ray of sunshine, piercing a darkness we ourselves may not dream is there.

The way in which power works is a mystery. As Schweitzer put it:

I look back upon my youth and realize how so many people gave me help, understanding, courage, meant something important to me—and they never knew it. They entered into my life and became powers within me. All of us live spiritually by what others have given us, often unwittingly, in the significant hours of our life. At the time these significant hours may not even be perceived. We may not recognize them until years later when we look back, as one remembers some long-ago music or a boyhood landscape. We all owe to others much of gentleness and wisdom that we have made our own; and we may well ask ourselves what will others owe to us.

No one can guess what effect his own life produces, nor calculate what he gives to others; that is hidden from us and must remain so, although we are often allowed to see some little fraction of it so that we may not lose courage.

Here an uncomfortable doctrine begins to prompt us. You are happy, it says. Therefore you are called to give up much. Whatever you have received more than others in health, in talents, in ability, in success, in a pleasant childhood, in harmonious conditions of home life—all this you must not take to yourself as a matter of course. You must pay a price for it. You must render in return some sacrifice of your life for other life.

This voice of the true ethic is dangerous for the happy, when they have the courage to listen to it. It challenges them to see whether they can make themselves adventurers of self-sacrifice, of whom the world has too few.

For those who have suffered in special ways, there are special opportunities, as, for example, the fellowship of those who bear the mark of pain. Those who have known what bodily anguish can mean belong together all the world over. If you have been delivered from pain, you must not think you are free. Never again can you be entirely forgetful of the past. From that moment on you feel bound to help to bring others to deliverance. If an operation has saved you from death or torture, do your part to make it possible for the kindly anesthetic and the helpful knife to begin their work in some other place where, until now, death and agony still rule unhindered. So with the mother whose child has been saved, and the children whose father's last torment was made tolerable by a doctor's skill; all must join in seeing to it that others may also know those blessings.

In renunciation and sacrifice we must give, most of all, of ourselves. To hand ten dollars to someone who needs it is not a sacrifice if you can well afford the money. The widow's mite was worth more than all the rich men's donations, because her mite was her all. In our own ways we must give something that it is a wrench to part with, if it is only time from the cinema, from favorite games, or from our other pleasures. Only by feeling the sacrifice can we know that we are giving of ourselves.

I hear people say:

"Oh, if I were only rich, I would do great things to help people."

But we all *can* be rich, in love and generosity, with what we have to give. Schweitzer once put this example to a young French housewife:

"Suppose at church on Sunday morning you were

handed one thousand francs to give to the poor. What would you do with it? If you were both wise and good, you would be careful; you would not toss the money away. No, you would make inquiries in the neighborhood. Who were the most needy? How much would suffice for them? You wouldn't give more than was necessary, because others also are in need. In finding the facts, you would be giving not only one thousand francs but your own loving interest and concern, which is worth more than all the money in the world.

"And by some working of the universal law, as you give of love you are given more money to go on with! Mysterious, but true!"

That is why charity, when dehumanized, can never do a proper job. Welfare work is, of course, necessary; we must have many and large charitable organizations. But the gaps must be filled by personal service, performed with loving kindness. A charitable organization is a complex affair; like an automobile, it needs a broad highway on which to run. It cannot penetrate the little bypaths; those are for men and women to walk through, with open eyes and hearts full of comprehension and pity. The greatest lack of all such organizations today is in workers who will give of themselves, professionals with seeing hearts.

We cannot abdicate our conscience to an organization, nor to a government. Cain's question is still important: "Am I my brother's keeper?" Most certainly I am! I cannot escape my responsibility by saying the bureaus of the state will do all that is necessary. It is a tragedy that there is a tendency nowadays to think and to feel otherwise.

Even in family life children are coming to believe they do not have to take care of the old folks. But old-age pensions are only to assist them in their tasks, not to relieve them of their duties. To dehumanize such care is wrong, because it abolishes the principle of love, which is, in its essence, a reverence for life and part of the foundation principle of the universe.

This does not mean merely reverence for human beings; not just an ethic for persons; if our love does not take in *all* living things, but only people, then we have a house without a foundation.

We have to teach our babies to be kind. Like Schweitzer's friends, the aborigines in French Equatorial Africa, children have a naïve cruelty, but they can learn to be merciful. For example, if the Africans are going to kill a goat for a feast, they will tie the poor creature's heels together and string him up, letting him hang from a tree in prolonged agony, instead of hitting him on the head and getting it over with. But they can learn better, as they did one time in Lambaréné, when Schweitzer and his helpers were putting up a new shed.

At the bottom of the newly dug post holes they found snails and toads and other tiny creatures. The workmen were about to set the first pole in place, and then drive it down with sledges. Of course the little living things would thereupon be smashed to death. With a wave of his hand the missionary motioned the workmen back and, kneeling at the hole, lifted out each moist, squirming creature and set it safely free. His concern for those tiny lives not only stunned the workmen, but delighted them. Later in the day, when a European nurse came out to take over the job, she started in to repeat the first mistake, but the tribesmen set up a great hallooing and stopped the massacre!

Reverence for life begins far down; tenderness toward

the weakest strengthens the heart toward life itself. We do terrible things to each other because we do not have comprehension and pity. The moment we understand and feel sorry for the next man, forgive him, we wash ourselves, and it is a cleaner world.

But why must I forgive my fellow man? Schweitzer answers that:

Because, if I do not forgive everyone, I shall be untrue to myself. I shall then be acting as if I were innocent of the same offenses, and I am not. I must forgive lies directed against me, because so many times my own conduct has been blotted by lies. I must forgive the lovelessness, the hatred, the slander, the fraud, the arrogance which I encounter, since I myself have so often lacked love, and have hated, slandered, defrauded and been arrogant. And I must forgive without noise or fuss. In general, I do not forgive; I do not even get as far as being merely just. But he who tries to live by this principle, simple and hard as it is, will know the real adventures and triumphs of the soul, for here is a mighty challenge.

A man has done us a wrong. Are we to wait for him to ask our forgiveness? No, no! He may never ask pardon, and then we shall never forgive, which is evil. No, let us simply say instead: "It does not exist!"

In a railway station I watch a man with dustpan and broom, sweeping up refuse in the waiting room. He cleans up a portion, then moves on to the next. But let him look back over his shoulder, and he will behold a man throwing a cigar stump on the floor, a child tearing paper and scattering it around—more litter accumulating where a moment before he had it all swept clean. Yet he has to go right on with his work and feel no rage. So must we all! In my personal relations with people I must never be without my pan and broom. I must clean up the litter. If the leaves do not drop off the trees in autumn, there will be no room for new leaves in the spring.

You think it is a wonderful life for Albert Schweitzer and his wife to live in the equatorial jungle? It is a more wonderful life to stay where you are, and put your soul to the test in a thousand little trials, and win triumphs of love. Such a career of the spirit demands patience, devotion, daring. It calls for strength of will and the determination to love: the greatest test of a man. But in this hard "second job" is to be found the only true happiness. As Goethe said:

"We must all pity each other."

"And truly," Schweitzer adds, "whenever I have given myself out in any way for another, I have experienced union with the eternal. And so I possess a cordial which secures me from dying of thirst in the desert of life."

4

THERE IS SOMETHING FOR YOU TO DO

*E*ven when people hear the challenging views of Dr. Schweitzer, and his homely examples of personal service, they are reluctant to believe that they can achieve any worth-while results. To such skeptics I generally hand a copy of the Reverend James Keller's famous book, *You Can Change the World*. There is in this book a treasury of histories, tales of men and women who, fired with zeal to be of use in the struggle for a better world, have dared to believe with the ancient Chinese that it is better to light one candle than to curse the darkness.

In a small California town a young Negro studying to be a teacher took a part-time job at a filling station to help support himself and his wife until he got his degree. But some customers objected; they wanted to buy gasoline only from white men. The owner was about to fire the boy when a woman neighbor asked:

"How many customers will you lose if you stand by this fellow?"

"About eighteen. Maybe twenty."

"If I get you twenty new customers, will you keep him on?"

"You bet I will."

Not only did this aroused woman bring twenty new customers, but five more for good measure. She was a Christopher, one of a growing band of men and women united in the purpose to help change the world into a better place.

Some are Christophers without even knowing it. One morning recently I saw a small crowd gathered around a Park Avenue window. No one was looking at the diamonds and rubies in the jeweler's shop to the right, or at the furs to the left. What drew all to the window between?

Peering over the heads of the fascinated group, I beheld, framed in dark oak, the prayer of St. Francis of Assisi:

. . . *O Divine Master, grant that I may not so much seek to be consoled, as to console; to be understood, as to understand; to be loved, as to love* . . .

Why those lines were put in that shopwindow I never found out. But whoever put them there was at heart a Christopher, brilliantly showing how one single person could make strangers on the street forget, if only for a few minutes, their own selfish concerns and think of others.

What is a Christopher? He is one who believes in individual responsibility for the common good of all, and sets himself a specific job to do; an average man or woman ready to work and make personal sacrifices. It is literally astounding to learn the results that are being achieved singlehanded by people of faith and zeal.

Although under Catholic auspices, the Christopher movement embraces the welfare of, and numbers among its followers, Protestants, Jews, and those possessing no faith at all. The movement has no chapters, no committees, no meetings; there are no memberships and no dues. From a central office in New York occasional bulletins are mailed out to more than a hundred thousand interested persons; that is the sole unifying contact. Each in his own way becomes a distributor of changeless Truth in our changing times, believing that, alone and unaided, he has a post of his own in the war between good and evil. And he must believe in the power of himself, as an individual, to change the world.

How singlehanded efforts multiply power was symbolized at a patriotic meeting of one hundred thousand citizens jammed into Los Angeles Coliseum one starless night. Suddenly the speaker—it was Father Keller himself—startled the throng:

"Don't be afraid now. All the lights are going out."

In complete darkness he struck a match.

"All who can see this little light say 'Yes!' "

A deafening roar came from the audience.

"So shines a good deed in a naughty world. *But suppose now every one of us here strikes a light!*"

Faster than it takes to tell, nearly one hundred thousand pinpricks of flame flooded the arena with light—the result of one hundred thousand individuals, each doing his own part. That is how the Christopher movement works.

Never was there a more spectacular indication of this theory than in the strange case of the Soviet schoolteacher.

When a woman jumped, one summer's day, from a high window of the Russian consulate in New York, the crash of her body on the pavement was heard around the world. But at that time the world heard only a part of the truth.

No outsider knew that Madame Oksana Stepanova Kasenkina would never have taken that spectacular leap if a young Connecticut farm wife and her brother, a novice lawyer, had not first intervened in an affair that seemed to be no business of theirs. This brother and sister set in motion a chain of events whose climax did more than anything else, before or since, to bring home to Americans the reality of Soviet duplicity and ruthlessness.

Now, with their permission, the story can be told.

It begins in a farmhouse at Ridgefield, Connecticut, on August 8, 1948, a sultry Sabbath morning.

Home from early church, the family surrounded the breakfast table, where Daniel McKeon was dividing Sunday comics among the children. Louise, blond young wife and mother, scanned the New York *Times*. "A terrible thing is happening!" she suddenly exclaimed, and read aloud from the front page. On Saturday a fifty-two-year-old widow had been kidnaped by Soviet officials from an estate near Nyack.

"Just listen to what went on!" gasped Louise.

Ten days before, Madame Kasenkina, in this country to teach the children of Russian delegates to the United Nations, had been ordered to return to Moscow. Her passage was arranged on the Soviet steamship *Pobeda*. Instead of going aboard, she hid herself. When the vessel sailed without her, she fled for protection to Valley Cottage, home of the anti-Communist Countess Alexandra Tolstoy, aging daughter of the great novelist. Madame Kasenkina's purpose was to remain in the United States and become a citizen. But Soviet raiders pounced on her sanctuary, and now it was feared she was being shanghaied to Russia, to be liquidated.

These accusations were denied. According to Jacob M. Lomakin, Soviet consul general, who now was holding the woman under "protection" in his New York house, he had merely "rescued" her from bondage in the household of Countess Tolstoy. Known to newsmen as a churlish fellow, the dour-faced Lomakin was today all smiles. He protested that he wanted everybody to know the whole truth.

Reporters crowding his office were introduced to a pale-faced woman garbed in black, with red rings around her brown eyes. Lomakin said:

"Here is Madame Oksana Stepanova Kasenkina. She came with us willingly. She wants to go to Russia."

These assertions were obsequiously confirmed by the woman herself. To experienced newspapermen, however, her assent seemed only an act of terrified obedience. They noticed her uneasy glances, her frightened air and plucking hands.

On that humid Sunday morning this same ugly news story was being read in millions of safe American homes, yet it did not occur to any of us that we should or could do anything about it.

But Louise McKeon, looking across at her husband, was deeply moved.

"Prisoners of Russian officials always agree with their jailers. There are horrible ways of making people do that. I believe that woman is really going to her death."

"Probably," agreed her husband.

"Won't anything be done about it?"

"Well, after all, that consulate is technically Soviet territory——"

"Why don't *we* do something about it?" blazed Louise.

Dan McKeon blinked in astonishment. A new light was shining in his wife's eyes, a glow of dedication. With all her duties as mistress of a large house, mother of six children, and with club and church obligations besides, why was Louise McKeon thus suddenly on fire? As the explanation dawned on him, Dan smiled. This was what had come of their recent talk with one of their oldest friends—Father James Keller. He had told them that people can, by selfless acts, bring about extraordinary changes in the world.

"But what can I do?" Louise had asked Father Keller. "A busy housewife, buried in Connecticut, can't help change the world."

"I don't care if you are buried in Alaska," Keller had replied. "Drop that feeling of personal futility and just try something sometime. When you do you will not be alone; the Good Lord will be right there helping you."

And now, on this Sunday morning, Dan McKeon realized that for his wife this moment was her "sometime," and that she was going to try something!

"But what can you or I possibly do in a case like this?" he argued. "Only the State Department can deal with Soviet Russia."

"Just the same, I'm going to do *something!*" cried Louise.

Dan McKeon rose and put his arms around her. "All right, darling, I'm with you," he said. "Now, let's see—what could we do? . . . Why not talk to your brother about it? Pete's a lawyer. And he's coming up from New York today."

Now Peter W. Hoguet was a very new lawyer. Only a year out of law school, he had just recently passed the state bar examinations. When he arrived at the McKeons' home they found that he was as indignant as they about the Kasenkina case. However, he didn't see that there was anything he could do.

"But no American could kidnap another American and

get away with it, could he?" Louise argued. "Are Russians allowed to break our laws?"

"Sis, it's not *our* business."

Louise McKeon's retort was a searching question: *"Well, if it's not our business, whose business is it?"*

Peter Hoguet shrugged and gave no answer—then. But on Monday night, as he rode the train back to Manhattan, the question would give him no peace: *"If it's not our business, whose business is it?"* Tuesday morning he dropped in on a friend, an experienced attorney.

"Women get queer ideas, don't they?" Peter began off-handedly, and told of his sister's excitement.

But the other man exclaimed: "She's right. Whose business is it—if not yours?"

From that moment young Peter Hoguet found his days a living melodrama.

First he decided to rely on a principle in law older than the Magna Charta—the habeas corpus (that you have the body), which is the right of any citizen believing that another is illegally detained to bring that person into a court of justice where the facts may be ascertained.

Rather than sue alone for such a writ, it would be more impressive, Peter felt, for him to appear as representative of some patriotic organization. Accordingly he went to Christopher Emmet, of Common Cause, Inc. With Mr. Emmet's co-operation the application was drawn, and on Wednesday afternoon Peter Hoguet held his first professional conversation with a judge in chambers; to Justice Samuel Dickstein of the New York Supreme Court he offered papers alleging that a woman was being held against her will in the Russian consulate "through power, deceit and terror being exercised upon her."

So cogent were his arguments that when he left he clutched a document commanding Jacob M. Lomakin, Soviet consul general, to be in Manhattan Supreme Court at Foley Square at 10 A.M. the following morning, Thursday, and to have with him "the body of Oksana Stepanova Kasenkina by you detained and imprisoned, as it is said."

Now all Peter had to do was to lay hands on Lomakin, one of the most elusive men in New York. He studied newspaper photographs to fix in memory the image of his quarry—lean, pale face; jutting, clifflike brow; eyes like deep cisterns, almost empty of light.

In legal protocol a lawyer of record does not serve his own summons. So Peter called a friend, another young lawyer, Hugh Donohue, New York commander of the Veterans of Foreign Wars.

Their rendezvous was the lobby of the Hotel Pierre at Fifth Avenue and Sixty-first Street, across the street from the stately marble-front mansion occupied by the Soviet consular staff. Almost at the instant of their arrival, as if unseen forces were already helping, a black limousine drew up before the consulate, and a lean, pale man with jutting forehead sprang to the sidewalk.

"Lomakin!" cried Peter. The writ was in his pocket; no time now to pass it to Donohue; legal etiquette would have to go hang. Peter ran across the street as a cluster of reporters deployed around the Russian consul. Furious at the ambuscade, Lomakin raked his pockets and belabored his own doorbell; lucklessly for him he was without a key. Peter sprang up the marble steps, brandishing his paper.

"Mr. Lomakin? This is a writ of habeas corpus for Mrs. Kasenkina."

Lomakin locked his hands behind his back. But Peter pushed the court summons down inside the consul's buttoned coat. Lomakin seized the detested thing to throw it into the street, and that angry act betrayed him; the order of the court was in his hands.

"Mr. Lomakin," exclaimed Peter, mopping his face, "you are now served. I'll meet you in court."

At ten o'clock next morning the youthful attorney appeared in Foley Square. He, who had never before had a case, found himself surrounded by cameramen. In the courtroom he assembled his witnesses. Countess Tolstoy and her associates from Valley Cottage. But where were Lomakin and Madame Kasenkina? Would the Russian official disregard an order of the New York Supreme Court?

When Justice Dickstein appeared on the bench, Peter Hoguet arose and announced: "Your honor, I am ready to proceed."

But Russia was not ready. Indeed, it looked as if Peter Hoguet was beating his head against an iron curtain. In Washington the Russian Ambassador, Alexander S. Panyushkin, had declared that the "entirely inadmissible assumption" that Lomakin could forcibly detain Madame Kasenkina was "incompatible with the dignity" of the consular office. And the United States Department of State had telegraphed Governor Thomas E. Dewey, suggesting that Justice Dickstein defer further action. To this plea Justice Dickstein agreed for two wholly sensible reasons:

1. Word had been received from Lomakin that he needed time to consult with his embassy. Under the fair play of American courts he was to be given that time.

2. There was need to consult with the State Department on whether Madame Kasenkina had been brought to this country under diplomatic privileges or as a mere consular employee. That technical point might determine the whole issue.

What the judge did not know—nor did Hoguet—was that a Soviet ship was to sail at midnight of this same Thursday; within a few hours Madame Kasenkina was to be shipped out. Then the habeas corpus writ could never be enforced.

Madame Kasenkina knew that she was to be a passenger on that ship. While Peter Hoguet stood glum and forlorn in court, the pallid woman in the case was being held in a third-floor room of the house on Sixty-first Street.

Through an open window came the noises of the city: cars, trucks, the shrill voices of children in Central Park nearby. Fantail pigeons fluttered on her window sill, but Stepanova did not see. Overcome with lassitude, lost in a mental cloud land, she slumped in a rocking chair. She has told friends that she scarcely heard the music coming from a portable radio on the bureau. If guards had suspected that Madame Kasenkina understood a little English, there would, of course, have been no radio in the room.

Madame Kasenkina's mind had gone back to the year 1937. In those days she was a teacher in a biological institute in Moscow, and her husband was also a science teacher. In the middle of night heavy blows on the front door aroused them from sleep; Soviet troopers broke in, seized her husband, and dragged him off. She never saw him again; never even learned his offense.

From that moment Madame Kasenkina dreamed of escape from the Soviet Union. But she had guilefully concealed her hope as she played the role of a fanatical servant of the totalitarian state. At last she had been brought to the United States. She had determined never to go back to Russia. Yet here she was, trapped like an animal—and, so she believed, no one, anywhere, cared what happened to her.

Presently she stood up and walked to the window. Looking out toward the street, she saw a sight that startled her, even in her misty state of mind. A crowd was staring at the front of her prison house. Police had to hold them back. What had brought all those people here? She must try to understand, try to clear her head. Last night a nurse had come to her bedside, thrust a needle into her arm, spurting into her veins the narcotic often used by Soviet police. Under its influence the mind of the drugged person becomes a dream world and all resolution fails; it was the purpose of the drug, Madame Kasenkina has stated, to break her will.

Still blear-eyed from the dose, confused when she so desperately wanted to think, Madame Kasenkina swayed dizzily toward the bathroom. She fumbled with the cold-water spigot, bent over and splashed the chilly stream over head and cheeks. Now she began to think more clearly. Again she started toward the window when she heard a voice from the radio uttering her name! What was the man saying, the newscaster with the excited voice? Intently she listened, hearing her name repeated, mispronounced but unmistakable. She was overpowered with emotion. She could translate a little part, at least, of what she heard.

There had been court action on her behalf! This news rekindled courage in her mind and soul. Now she knew why crowds filled the street below. She was not abandoned;

the fate of an individual still meant something in America. *Somebody had tried; somebody did care! All those people cared!*

In that ineffable moment of realization Madame Kasenkina was inspired to a sacrifice that might blazon the truth unmistakably to the people. There was in her mind no thought of self-destruction. In her belief, suicide could not be justified. Instead, there was a growing faith that she might dare to do a dangerous thing to prove the truth, and live to serve it. She turned resolutely to the open window. Leaning far out on the projecting ledge, she looked down three stories to the concrete pavement of a walled-in yard. It was a moment of decision. Two floors below she saw a telephone line strung across the court. She aimed her body at that wire to break the fall and save her life—and then she jumped. The wire, though it nearly severed her hand, broke her fall and saved her life.

All America knows the rest of the story. From a bed in Roosevelt Hospital the crippled Madame Kasenkina was a more effective witness against tyranny than she ever could have been on a witness stand. And with what world-stirring results!

Consul General Lomakin had to leave this country in disgrace. Other officials were also called home. In the pillory of international news, they, and the mighty Molotov with them, had been exposed as arrant liars. Not only in the United States, but throughout Europe, the Kasenkina case galvanized public opinion against Soviet lawlessness.

Today Louise McKeon knows that her old friend, Father Keller, was right; that a single individual can set in motion far-reaching events. The pattern of her brother's life is altered too. Putting aside his ambition to have a lucrative practice, Peter Hoguet has dedicated his career to opposing injustice.

And Madame Kasenkina? Wounds and broken bones largely healed, she now lives in retirement in a lonely corner of Long Island. Never again can she feel alone; for she is one in spirit with all those who, like herself, would offer to die that freedom may live.

5

THE ZEAL OF THE CHRISTIAN

*T*HERE is always the danger that zeal may outrun common sense, and that is something to guard against.

Zeal without knowledge has been called the sister of folly. Dean Swift once estimated the odds at a hundred to one that violent zeal for the truth would prove to be either petulancy, ambition, or pride. Justice Louis D. Brandeis, in an opinion of the Supreme Court of the United States, wrote that the greatest dangers to liberty lurk in insidious encroachment by men of zeal, well meaning but without understanding. But the eminent jurist failed to take into account also the possibilities of well-meaning men *with* understanding. He might have gone much further and spoken with broader wisdom.

Nevertheless, his opinion did anticipate today's lugubrious spectacle, where many so-called liberals seem willing to support a tyranny of reform far more evil than the wrongs they would like to cure. Surely we have all seen enough misguided energy to make us cautious; that was why Talleyrand said: *"Surtout, pas du zèle!* [Above all, no zeal!]"

Especially are realistic people mistrustful of religious

fervor. Some confidently expect that a man, really filled with the Holy Spirit, will turn into a whirling dervish, or a rolling epileptic. Even when the earnest Christian preserves an outward semblance of propriety and reasonableness and good will, the intellectual is privately sure that someday, like a volcano, he is bound to erupt.

It is hard for the conservative to believe that a man, filled with the spirit of worship and service, may be *more* understanding, *more* forgiving, *more* full of love, *more* sensible than the confused, the bewildered, the sick at heart, the frustrated and the spiritual coward, whose countenance is sicklied o'er with the pale cast of thought.

What *is* true is that the sensible, good-willed man of conviction is nevertheless ready, not only to live by his principles but to die for them. If zeal of that sort is fanaticism, let this listless age make the most of it.

Unafraid, at the opening of the Old Testament cave, Elijah answered the mysterious Voice by saying:

"I have been very jealous for the Lord God of hosts: for the children of Israel have forsaken Thy covenant, thrown down Thine altars, and slain Thy prophets with the sword; and I, even I only, am left; and they seek my life, to take it away."

And, like Elijah, the true follower of God's voice today is willing that his life be taken away, when nothing less will do.

The skeptical world knows this and it fears most of all the zeal of the Christian. The immoralists, the materialists, the Communists, dread the power of Christianity in action; but they know, too, that they are safe so long as that power is held in leash by complacency, smugness, or laziness. If every Christian would assert his belief, not only by reciting a creed, but by public action, the complexion of this world would soon lose its fever hue of red.

The harvest is still great, but the laborers are still few.

What our crazy world needs is not merely more hospitals, more pensions, more treaties, more hydrogen bombs. What is needed, desperately and immediately, is a renewal of zeal in every Christian soul, the rededication of our years, the consecration of all that we possess to our faith in God.

Remember the story of Nicodemus, rich ruler in Israel, coming in the darkness to inquire of the Master himself the meaning of His message. Ready and eager to learn, the ancient millionaire was baffled when he was flatly told that he must be born again. All Christians face that implacable requirement. But who that has been born again, who that in darkness has found the light, can remain silent, or restrain his overmastering eagerness to spread the good news?

And would anyone counsel him to keep his transforming experience to himself? Who would not expect him to be apostolic now, at least in his heart, if not in his achievements? The question is answered in the Apocalypse, the Bible's Book of Revelation; Almighty God, speaking to all who claimed to follow Him:

"I would thou wert cold, or hot. But because thou art lukewarm, and neither cold, nor hot, I will begin to vomit thee out of my mouth. . . . Be zealous, therefore, and do penance."

So we have our marching orders straight from the throne of grace. With the sense of responsibility that thus falls upon souls, can we possibly have a moment's doubt that a resurgence of Christian ardor is the one hope left for mankind?

Once we look at the problem in historical perspective, the issue today becomes hideously clear. As Dr. Elton D. Trueblood, of Earlham University, has pointed out, in his book, *The Predicament of Modern Man*, what we know as Western culture, and the ideals and realities and achievements of freedom and faith which we cherish, all stem from the Judaeo-Christian culture which was born long ago in the Holy Land. Out of that plan for man's redemption has grown the glory of the modern world. The political, scientific, and artistic flowering of all the centuries since is the product of the Old and the New Testaments, the undying truths of the Ten Commandments and the Sermon on the Mount.

But in spite of that flowering of civilization there appeared in the days of our grandfathers a new heresy, a brash apostasy that stemmed from uncompleted scientific research. The little knowledge of those researchers was a dangerous thing. Drawing wholly unwarranted conclusions from Darwin, hearkening to the crass materialistic fallacies of Haeckel and the atavistic counsel of Nietzsche, people began to say: "Now we see that religion is only superstition. Revelation is fraudulent. Only men of second-rate minds can believe such stuff any longer."

Then it was that the whole world of secular education turned its face away from faith. But not as quickly did thoughtful men turn away from moral principles. "No," they said, "we will drop the old religion, but we will hold onto the old ethical code."

Mankind has always been overproduced on ethical codes. But how seldom do they fire the human heart to martyrdom. There is nothing in this world so jejune, so lifeless, as an ethical code. It is the letter that kills, as Jesus assured us.

Meanwhile, the disease of heresy was spreading into political philosophy. Marx wrote his textbook of selfishness and force, and from that myopic volume was hatched what we know today as Communism. It filled with flummery, flapdoodle, and fanaticism a void left in the brains of men when faith was cast out. Because man is incurably religious, he must have some kind of vision or perish. Many times in history he has served a false faith with cruel and pleasurable excitement. So it is today. Such, in all honesty, is the plight of every Communist. The Communist is filled with fanatical zeal. He is maddened with the energies of his fierce hatreds, his puerile fears. Thus he is possessed of unresting, galvanic, destructive force, and thus we are confronted with a dangerous paradox.

In the West we stand, millions of us, confused and listless: ethics without zeal. In the East, behind the Iron Curtain, there stand millions of armed fanatics: zeal without ethics.

Can there be any doubt which will be victorious—the indifferent or the zealous?

That is why, as never before in history, our time calls for the complete and sacrificing consecration of Christians. Complacence is no longer tolerable. Smugness is now a deadly disease. Indifferentism is suicide of the soul. No Christian can any longer take religion quietly, as a matter of course. We are crusaders today—or we are corpses.

These are the days when man can travel faster than the speed of sound—yet he rushes in circles, getting nowhere.

Here at home, in intimate clarity, we see the general

moral collapse. On every hand modern man is worked upon by a stealthy and organized conspiracy, that, for its own necessities, is determined to break the tablets of the commandments and to ridicule out of intelligent respectability the teachings of the Sermon on the Mount. More and more, man is being deluded and betrayed by that conspiracy.

Never as now has the battle between good and evil been so frankly drawn. This is not a new war; it is the oldest of wars. It began in Eden and will not end until Armageddon.

In many American homes helpless parents meet its victims face to face in irreconcilable family clashes. Bring up your child in the way he should go, but once he is beyond your doorstep, out in the world by himself, every virtuous principle you have taught him becomes a target for the enemies of Christianity.

It is the fashion today to blame everything on Communism, but if Stalin died tonight, and all his comrades with him; if the Iron Curtain were lifted at dawn and all the people were free from the purges and slavery and liquidation and the rule of the lie, we would still be faced with the basic, world-wide conflict between good and evil.

And if there were no more Communists working to destroy religion and freedom in the United States, our children would still come back to us with those same denials of what we have taught them.

Not Communism, but godlessness, the dragon mother of Nazism, Fascism, *and* Communism, has brought us to this pass.

In the presence of monstrous disorder on the earth, we must, therefore, have zeal, or else wait without hope for chaos.

Thank God we have before us illustrious examples to promise us again the supernatural assurance that zeal for Christ begets spiritual power and spiritual power begets victory.

Who can doubt that Cardinal Mindszenty's persecution, which has brought him also to servitude, has in its cruel injustice called millions, once indifferent, back to their knees? The unshaken ardor of such men is a tocsin to the sleeping conscience of mankind. Like the Maccabees of old, they are sounding the alarm.

I truly believe that we—all Christians—must imitate, in our own sphere of opportunity, these brave servants of God.

In doing so we shall make mistakes—yes. There are dangers that go with every form of dynamic energy. It is easy to make fools of ourselves. But St. Paul calls upon us to be fools for Christ's sake. Our own unguided efforts can easily lead to disaster. By our ineptitude we can bring scandal to our cause. Therefore, we must pray for guidance, and, therefore, work with careful and experienced counsel. It is the tendency of the overzealous to go off half cocked. It is a part of God's wisdom that we have mentors, to be the engineers of our steam and to see that we don't blow up the boiler.

Having that guidance in all that we do, where, then, shall we begin? Where but in our own lives?

The power of example in one Christian life, however humble and obscure, is beyond all calculation. Here our problems are clear but staggering; we must merely perform the simple duties of a Christian. But when we begin to contemplate those duties, we may well wonder if there is time enough in life to do anything else.

Gilbert Chesterton once said that Christianity has not, as so many suppose, been tried and found a failure. It has been found hard and not tried. There is not one of us who does not shrink from a cross. To practice Christian doctrine is the challenge of a lifetime.

Who of us can easily obey those Ten Commandments for twenty-four hours?

And they are not even a beginning. We can never begin without a knowledge that we shall be divinely helped in our efforts; more than anything else we need a sense of the supernatural. We must realize that we are living in direct contact with universal love and power and truth—and we must conduct ourselves accordingly. That sense of supernatural assistance is the indispensable equipment of the zealous Christian.

To all the earnest, well-intentioned, earth-bound do-gooders of today I say that it is not enough to build the most modern hospitals, necessary as they are. The finest of those hospitals is a failure and a denial of Christ if there is not space within it, and time within it, for healing prayers. Just as surely as Jesus cured paralytics and lepers, so today there is no disease so horrible that it cannot be cured without knife or drug, but by faith in Him alone.

How strange a thing it is to listen to modern jargon about such things. If, on the street, we were to come upon some miserable wretch groveling on the floor, foaming at the mouth, and then follow him to a neurological clinic; if we were to listen to the diagnosis, we would perhaps hear the psychiatrist say: "This man is suffering from ambivalence. He is a schizophrene." Doctor, what does that mean? "It means the man has two personalities at war within himself." I see, Doctor. What did Jesus say?

He said the man had a devil.

What did that mean? It meant that he was possessed. Possessed of what? Possessed, not of schizophrenia, but of a veritable devil. Of two warring personalities. Isn't that right?

But there are two points of difference. Almost never can the psychiatrist cure his schizophrene, whether it be a mere mental case or a case of possession, disease or demon. But Jesus is able to heal such a man instantly and infallibly, with a power equally available in all ages.

Recently I talked with a famous psychiatrist who confided to me that, while he was an atheist, his best cures of the mentally ill came through religion. He told me the only way he could cure many of his patients was by appealing to their faith in God and insisting on their surrender to God's will. Surrender—not submission, he emphasized. When a man submits to the inevitable, he still has a gleam in his eye and he is saying to himself, "My time will come. I will get even for this." That attitude is a passport to permanent insanity.

The same psychiatrist assured me that grudges, resentments, hatreds, and fears are crazy seeds that flower in the mind. Only when grudges are thrown away like weeds, when the heart is cleansed of resentments and the soul is filled with forgiveness and full co-operative surrender to the will of God, can the mentally ill find recovery and peace. Where are such things to be found? On the couch of the psychoanalyst? Never. We will find them only at the altar.

When we are there we are at the true beginning of Christian duty, the door to personal opportunities for zeal. Who of us can examine his conscience today and say:

"I have admonished the sinner, instructed the ignorant, counseled the doubtful, comforted the sorrowful; I have borne wrongs patiently, I have forgiven all injuries, I pray for the living and the dead"? Who among us has given not merely contributions to worthy causes but enough of our time to feed the hungry, to give drink to the thirsty, to clothe the naked, ransom the captive, harbor the harborless, visit the sick, and bury the dead?

Can we say that we have earned the blessings promised to the poor in spirit, the meek, they that mourn, they that hunger and thirst after justice, the merciful, the clean of heart, the peacemakers and the persecuted?

How many of us have succeeded in cutting pride out of our lives, to replace it with humility; covetousness with liberality, lust with chastity, anger with meekness, envy with brotherly love, gluttony with temperance, and sloth with diligence?

And how many of us have remembered what are the four sins of such infernal wickedness that they cry to Heaven for vengeance? Willful murder? Oh, yes. The sin of Sodom? Yes, we cringe from all profanation. But the other two? Let them stand as the answer to all the revolutionary detractors of the Christian faith. Oppression of the poor is one. Defrauding laborers of their wages is the other.

Communism was seeded by transgressions of those laws. Communism is more than a philosophy which we reject with all our souls. Communism is a criticism. If Christians had had the zeal to live up to the teachings of their faith, such a criticism could never have been made.

But this program for the individual, strenuous and difficult though it may be, is still not nearly sufficient. The Christian life is partial if it is merely a system of do-good calisthenics. We have our part to play in changing the world. There are things that every one of us can do.

One of them is to keep ourselves informed; to take an interest in what is going on, especially as it affects the moral atmosphere of our country. We can begin at any time to be active citizens of a republic that was founded on a belief in the Father of Lights. We can shake off our inertia; we can take the trouble to learn the name of our congressional representative, our senator, and our state legislators. When something is wrong, we can write a letter of protest. Let no one tell you such protests go unregarded; they are carefully considered because they represent votes.

The practical opportunities for the zealous Christian are limited only by his own willingness. The practical work that the zealous Christian can perform is limited only by his resourcefulness.

They say that new brooms sweep clean. Let us hope so. If we do not clean up the debris of the world, Satan and his angels will make a clean sweep.

Surely, then, we can agree that zealousness, governed by prayer and guidance, is a good thing, a necessary thing; and that the need of the day is for all Christians to rally to our cause with ardor ten times greater than that of our foes. In our prayers, in our lives, let us be saturated with the love of God; let us pray for grace, for strength, and for opportunity. God will never fail the faithful. If, then, we are faithful, how can we fail?

6

THE WISE AND THE HARMLESS

*T*HE antidote to reckless zeal was given us by Jesus, who said we must be as wise as serpents and as harmless as doves. Often we must use a serpentine wisdom in this practical world, even to accomplish results that most people of good will most heartily approve of. We have to take account of the prejudices, the inertia, the actual bad will in the world—and make progress in spite of it.

Let me tell you a true story of a friend of mine who knew how to be cunning as well as kind. His zeal was dynamite; as one small stick of explosive, strategically placed, can clear away tons of rock, so the sophisticated Christianity of my friend actually helped to change the face of our time. It began in his office, which was in Brooklyn. It is the story of another man who knows there is a God and who has done God's work in a very strange field indeed.

The room was large and simply furnished, and there were two framed pictures on the wall. One was a Koda-chrome snapshot of a garrulous problem child of baseball. The other, hanging behind the paper-littered desk, was a rare collector's item, portrait of a prophet, the face trusting and full of faith.

It was that never-to-be-forgotten August 29 when our Marines landed on the soil of Japan; a day of blistering heat, with the clamor of traffic around Brooklyn's borough hall roaring through the open windows. Behind the desk stood Branch Rickey, owner of the Dodgers; facing him loomed a tall and powerful Negro, a perfectly muscled 185-pounder, with enormous hands and bold, bright eyes.

"Well, Jackie Robinson," began the baseball boss, "I suppose you know why I brought you here?"

"Of course, Mr. Rickey. You want me to play with your all-colored Brooklyn team."

Branch Rickey shook his head.

"No, Jackie. I brought you here to play for the Brooklyn Dodgers—if you can!"

For a moment the dark man's tongue was chained up without a sound. What he had just heard was almost beyond his belief. For all of seventy years there had been racial exclusion in big-league baseball, and, in spite of latter-day agitation and bitterness, conservatives still insisted that the game would speedily collapse if the color line were to be broken. No wonder this dark, large-boned athlete, tall and supple as a Zulu prince, could not believe his ears.

"Mr. Rickey, wouldn't that mean trouble ahead?" he asked in a small voice.

Hands in pockets, Rickey lounged against the front of the desk as he took time to look backward.

"I remember an old couple that took their first train ride when I was a boy. As they went through the mountains, the old man looked out of the window and wailed to his wife: 'Trouble ahead, Mom! Trouble ahead! We're high up over a precipice and we're going to run right off into space!' But the road curved into a tunnel and they came out all right. Now the reason they came out all right was that the road had been safely planned; it was an engineering job. And we're going to need plenty of engineering, you and I."

"You'd really dare to put a black boy on your team, Mr. Rickey?"

"But not because you're a black boy!" snapped Rickey sharply. "That would surely mean trouble. If I take you on, it's got to be because you're a ballplayer—and a good one."

In two exciting years Jackie Robinson was to learn that Branch Rickey's view of the problem transcended mere race antagonism; its roots lay deep in a simple faith that tact and tenacity can clear up any kind of human misunderstanding. First and foremost, because Rickey is a baseball fanatic, he wanted to find good new players.

Here in his office this hot Wednesday stood a very promising candidate, judged by his record alone: an ex-college student who had been a twenty-four-letter athlete. A religious boy, who neither smoked nor drank. And the only person, of any race, ever selected to play in college all-star games in both football and basketball.

Although Rickey had never seen him before, he knew his whole story; how he had been born in Cairo, Georgia, on the last day of January 1919, just when diplomats were sitting down to prepare their frightful blunders in the mirrored halls of Versailles. The family moved to California, where Jackie's mother, by doing housework, could send her two powerfully energetic boys to public school. (Jackie's brother, Mack, was later to set a world's record for sprinting and came in second to Jesse Owens at the Berlin Olympics in 1936.)

It was already clear that Jackie was an athletic prodigy. He starred in football, basketball, baseball, and track at the John Muir Technical High School in Los Angeles. By the time he was graduated in 1937 he had set a record for the running broad jump of 25 feet, 6½ inches. He made a basketball record of 28 points in one game in which he did not play full time. Again, in his second year at the University of California in Los Angeles, he led all the county football teams in yardage of punts returned, and had the highest batting average of all junior college baseball players with the fantastic record of .466. His spectacular performances admittedly raised the attendance records of the games.

But Rickey's scouts had inquired even farther, reporting that after a short period of practice Jackie Robinson had gone into tennis semifinals of a national competition. And the first time he ever swung a golf club he turned in a score of 99!

Rickey also knew that Jackie had left college in his junior year to support his mother. For a while he played professional football with the Los Angeles Bull Dogs. When he was drafted in 1942, army experts sent him forthwith to an officers' candidate school. By November he was a second lieutenant, and for thirty-one months he was overseas. Honorably discharged as first lieutenant, he had since been playing shortstop, doing sensational fielding for the Kansas City Monarchs, an all-black team where his batting average was .340.

Was such promising material to be barred from the big leagues?

"Jackie," resumed Branch Rickey, "there are a lot of hurdles for you. I've got to be sure you're really big league. But, above all, I've got to be sure that you can stand the gaff. Do you know what you're going to be up against? Look me in the eye, Jackie. I'm not Branch Rickey any more. Now I'm a hotel clerk in some lousy dump where they won't like you."

The change in the baseball manager was uncanny; the gruff, kindly face instantly turned into Simon Legree; hate crackling in angry eyes:

"You can't stay here in this white man's hotel! Trying to play on a white man's team! You want to be white? What you doing this for? Answer me!"

The dark chin went up. The big boy swallowed hard and then faltered:

"I don't want to be white. I just want to play big-league ball to prove to all the rest of our people that they've got a chance too."

Rickey whirled and walked across the room. When he turned again he was impersonating another un-pleasant character: a shoulder-swinging, forward-lurching tough.

"You get out of this white man's car. You belong in a Jim Crow car. You can't travel with white men. A nigger is a nigger, and that's all he'll ever be—just a nigger. Well, what've you got to say?"

A dangerous light flared up in Jackie Robinson's eyes. His fists were clenched; for a moment Rickey wondered if he was going to attack. Then the hands dropped.

"I don't want to make any trouble. I just came down here to play ball."

But then a sudden cry escaped him:

"Mr. Rickey, what do you have to say these things to me for?"

The manager laid a steadying hand on one prodigious shoulder.

"Because other people are going to say even worse things to you. And we can't fight prejudice man by man—there're too many. We can't just go out and prate and preach and crusade, and bust our heads against a brick wall. You're a Christian, Jackie, and you ought to know the Bible. The dear Lord once said we must be harmless as doves, but also wise as serpents. That means smart as a rattlesnake, without the venom. It's just good, simple Christianity for us to face realities, to recognize what we're up against, and to fight the problems with tact and common sense, good will and guts!"

The ballplayer replied:

"Mr. Rickey, anybody who says I can't take it doesn't know what I've already gone through and what I'm prepared to go through to make good. But can we win?"

The baseball magnate grabbed the player's arms.

"Sure, there'll be players from some Jim Crow states that'll get sore if you come on the team. They'll learn, because we'll teach them, not antagonize them. But, Jackie, haven't you got a little bit of a temper yourself?"

"Mr. Rickey," answered Robinson, "my temper is simply a beaut."

"I thought you were about to break me in half a few minutes ago. Now that's very serious. You're going to be the one man in baseball who can't lose his temper. You're not going to like all the umpires' decisions. Swallow them and grin. And all the insults. Because if you get in a brawl, Jackie, they won't just take it out on you—they'll stigmatize your people because of you. Out on the field you've got to be almost a saint. How're you going to manage that?"

"Only way I know to do," said Jackie, "is how my mother taught me. I've got to pray!"

From a drawer of his desk Branch Rickey now produced two blue-covered documents. They were not contracts. They were simply agreements in which Jackie Robinson promised to sign a contract if he should be offered one. But the terms were explicit. He was to be paid $600 a month if and when he was taken on—plus a bonus of $3500 in cash.

One thing was obvious: No one had to offer a cash bonus to entice Robinson into the big time. I asked Rickey why he included the bonus, and his answer was:

"Because I wanted the young man to feel like a ball-player."

"Better read the agreement all through," cautioned Rickey, and sat down to wait.

For this experiment he had waited a long time; he was no Johnny-come-lately to this risky innovation. There had been family conferences on the subject in the Rickey household for years, and always when they talked about the hazards, the father of the family had flared up with the faith of a zealot—a simple faith in God and people, and an unshakable loyalty to what he believed.

Baseball still remembers that incident in 1905 when Branch Rickey decided between principle and expediency. He had just been brought up from a Texas team to catch for the Cincinnati Reds. Five days after he joined, that famous manager and ex-Oriole, Joe Kelly, ordered him to play in the next day's game, upon which Rickey refused and turned over his mask and glove to another player.

Why? Because it was Sunday. His mother didn't like him to play on Sunday. Joe Kelly was apoplectic.

"You're in the big league now," he stormed. "For silliness like that would you get yourself fired?"

"If I have to, Mr. Kelly."

"Then go up and get your money now."

Which Branch Rickey did. His mother never knew that he stepped out of a great chance simply because he didn't want to hurt her. To this day he doesn't attend Sunday ball games.

As a climax to those family councils Rickey began, in 1943, a search for top-notch Negro talent. He was starting no crusade; controlling twenty-seven teams, he had to compete for players against wealthy rivals; here, perhaps, was a way to tap an untried source. He even started the all-Negro Brown Dodgers, but that was never a success. Meanwhile he sent scouts into Mexico, Cuba, and Puerto Rico, where there were no racial bans, and in that long hunt he spent more than $25,000.

Rickey's scouts had no idea what they were really looking for; they thought they were scouting for the Brown Dodgers. From the beginning Rickey followed the Bible's advice, not letting his right hand know, in addition to being wise as a serpent. By 1945 all the scouts were sending in reports about a certain Jackie Robinson, then playing with the Kansas City Monarchs at $500 a week.

It was just at a time when the racial controversy was boiling up. Sports writers were agitating the question, as were many Negro organizations. Governor Dewey had appointed a commission to forward the state's new anti-discrimination act. Mayor LaGuardia had formed his own anti-discrimination committee, and the secretary of that,

Dr. Dodson, was later to prove a helpful ally to Rickey. Suddenly a pamphlet was distributed all over Harlem by a Communist political candidate, the cover of which told a bitter story. Displayed there was an actual photograph of a dead Negro soldier lying in the mud. Opposite was a picture of a dark batsman, and below the legend read:

Good enough to die for his country, but not good enough for the big league.

Communist agitation? Certainly! But, alas, all too true! Everybody knew it was true, and politicians were scurrying around trying to find excuses, because elections were coming up. One big-name committee tried to quiet the agitation by declaring that nothing could be done until the Negro ball teams cleaned financial house. Rickey had to smile. When a colored team was forced to pay $100,000 a year rent for the use of a ball park, how could they ever have a healthy financial setup?

Word also came that a parade of protest was being organized. Thousands of Negroes carrying banners were to storm the Polo Grounds of the New York Giants, interrupting a game, demanding rights and inviting riot.

At that critical juncture the owners of the New York major clubs were called to a downtown conference. Larry MacPhail was there from the Yankees, Horace C. Stoneham from the Giants, and Rickey from the Dodgers. An official, who shall be nameless here, handed the three baseball magnates a typed announcement and crisply requested them to sign. The statement promised that "hereafter" these three managers would not discriminate against Negro players on their teams. Rickey dropped the paper on the desk, refusing to sign.

"But why, Mr. Rickey?"

"Because," was the answer, "I never *have* discriminated against any player for race, color, or creed. And I'll never hire a man for those reasons either!"

Now, months later, he offered a pen, and the player signed his full name—Jack Roosevelt Robinson. But as Rickey picked up his copy, he saw Robinson's great brown hand extended, holding out the other copy; the player's eyes fixed on the face in the framed picture above the manager's desk.

"Mr. Rickey," he said huskily, "I realize this is an important piece of paper. You better keep it for me."

Then the troubles began. A hush-hush meeting of certain powerful baseball personalities was called in the Middle West, at which a secret document was signed. It has never been published, but it recorded the conviction of those signers that the introduction of colored players on big-league teams would ruin all baseball investments.

Rickey did not attend that meeting; he had been busy signing up four other Negro players with equal secrecy. But he knew that the fate of his great experiment lay with the champion possibility, Jackie Robinson. Strengthened in that conviction, he took an airplane on October 23, 1945, to talk with the manager of his prize minor team of the International League. He had decided to put Robinson on the Montreal Royals and see what he would do in the season of 1946.

You can understand Branch Rickey's perturbation only when you remember that the manager of the Royals was Mr. Clay Hopper of the old Clay family and the old Hopper family in Greenwood, Mississippi. It was Rickey's task to convince this prince of good managers from the Yazoo

River country, where black people still sing at their work in the cotton fields, that *he* was chosen to break the color line!

The printable arguments of Mr. Hopper were that Rickey was overenthusiastic and ahead of his time. All night long the two men talked, but Rickey never budged from his position. His plans, he insisted, had nothing to do with race prejudice or agitation for tolerance. This was baseball, not race ball! Team spirit must come first.

And still being wise as a serpent, Rickey predicted that Robinson would prove a real attraction whose drawing power at the gate would increase the box-office receipts of the Montreal Royals. It would be idle pretense to say that Clay Hopper sang and danced with joy. Or that the players on the team threw up their hats and cheered. But it was decided to go ahead.

Meanwhile Robinson was busy with his own affairs. He had married Rachael Annetta Isum, a college graduate who had worked as a nurse in Los Angeles. Their honeymoon was being spent in Venezuela, where Jackie was playing on a barnstorming team. But in February he reported for spring training with the Royals at Daytona Beach, Florida.

Here again Rickey had given strict orders against looking for trouble. Their job was to get Jackie Robinson into baseball, not, for example, to make Jackie Robinson welcome in Daytona hotels. Someday hotel men would deal with their own problems. With no ructions, Jackie found quarters for himself. On the diamond he took the coach's orders and played ball.

When the time came for exhibition games, some were played on secondary fields, but two towns canceled because of protests against "mixed athletics," although the official reasons given were that one field was not in condition and the lights of the other had failed—which, in a spiritual sense, was certainly true.

No protest! Why battle with hostility to gain nothing? Courage and common sense and patience!

But there did come a big fly buzzing around Rickey. A certain Jorge Pasquel, major-domo of the Mexican League, was scattering thousand-dollar bills like autumn leaves to tempt American ballplayers below the border. Pasquel dearly wanted Robinson. He made a tempting offer at a time when Jackie had already felt many a stinging insult. No prejudice in Mexico, boasted Pasquel, and a large salary! But although Rickey had still not given him a contract, Jackie stuck to his bargain.

On April 18 in the Roosevelt Stadium at Jersey City Robinson played before a capacity crowd of twenty-five thousand, and that, as everybody knows, was probably the most extraordinary debut of any ballplayer.

There had never been anything quite like it before. Jackie batted .800. He scored four runs; he faultlessly handled six out of seven chances, and he helped in seven of the fourteen Montreal runs. He hit one home run, too, although he is not a long-distance hitter. There is a peculiarity to his swing of the bat which imparts a back spin to the ball. It goes up in a sharp trajectory and seems to hang, fabulously suspended, before it falls. But in that first New Jersey game he whammed the ball to the backfield. He made base hits and he stole bases, and the crowd roared.

For the next few weeks Jackie Robinson played rather poor baseball.

"I think I was trying too hard," he told me. "I was so

grateful for the chance—I felt it was so important for me to make good—that I got in my own way."

Already the fans liked him, but troubles were not over. They had yet to play my fine old native town of Baltimore. One night an important baseball official came to Rickey's home.

"Branch," he said, "we're playing Baltimore next week and the reports are very alarming. I'm deeply worried. Now don't try to calm me down. If you knew that Jackie Robinson would be killed next Monday afternoon, would you send him into that town with the team?"

"No," admitted Rickey, "I don't think I would."

"If you knew there was going to be a riot and maybe fifty people would be killed, would you send Jackie Robinson to Baltimore?"

"No," conceded Rickey.

"Well, that's what's going to happen."

"I don't believe it. You've been listening to a few loud-mouthed no-accounts. You know yourself that if I went into Baltimore tomorrow with Joe Louis fighting a white man I could pack the Fifth Regiment Armory. What makes baseball different from boxing?"

The Royals played Baltimore to a record grandstand and bleachers, and no trouble. Against all such fantasies Rickey opposed unfaltering faith. The result was that with Robinson as their great attraction the Montreal team's paid admissions on the circuit jumped to three times the preceding season. And long before the financial picture was clear, Clay Hopper had said to Branch Rickey:

"There is only one word for your black boy. He is okay."

Now what was Branch Rickey to do? A baseball man first and always, he looked at the record. When the season was over, Montreal had won the junior world series, and Arch Murray of the New York *Evening Post* wrote that Jackie Robinson "beat the powerful Louisville club all but singlehanded." In one season with the Royals Jackie had won the batting championship of the International League, with an average of .349; he had stolen 40 bases, had tied for scoring the most runs (113), and led the second basemen by fielding .985. In playing 119 games that season, more than 1000 innings, he had made only 10 errors.

Would Rickey put him on the big time at last? That question was in every fan's mind. But other questions were in Rickey's mind. How was Robinson's temper these days? This man of intense emotion, with such need for self-control, and still plagued by insulting exasperations every day of his life, every game he played—had he disciplined himself to endure what might happen if he came to the front line?

The tip-off came when Rickey announced that the Dodgers and Royals would train in the spring of 1947, not in Florida, but in Cuba, where there would be no race problem. Yet not many seemed to catch on; there was growing agitation for Robinson's promotion.

"Let the storm rise," said Rickey. "The more the public demands Jackie, the easier the trick will be."

Meanwhile, with Arthur Mann, expert sports author and his personal assistant, he was planning a finesse in public relations. These two men understood the hurdles yet to be overcome; their hope lay in the same old weapons of audacity, Christian good will, and common sense.

One night in coldest February a conclave was held in the Carlton Avenue branch of the Brooklyn colored

Y.M.C.A. Thirty-two Negro leaders of the borough sat down to dinner with Rickey, Mann, Judge Lazansky, and Dr. Dodson. Over cigars and coffee Rickey opened up:

"Gentlemen, at this moment I have still not decided whether Jackie Robinson will play for the Dodgers this season or not. But *if* he does, I will need your fullest co-operation. You cannot expect the white people to do it all. They must be co-operative, and so must you. One of the greatest hazards is the overenthusiasm of Negroes themselves. I mean, of course, the unthinking part of your people. Not wrong ones, mind you, but the overexcitable, boisterous ones who, by very excess of pride and excitement, may cause public tensions and clashes.

"That was why, when a special train was chartered in Buffalo to carry several thousand Negroes to Montreal to see Jackie play, we induced the organizers to cancel the trip. This young man's future is not as a Negro, but as a ballplayer—just as the future of all your people is not as Negroes, but Americans. Never think of Jackie as something different in this free land, but as actually belonging to it, just as I do.

"If he becomes a symbol of superior prowess in your race alone, the whole hope of getting forward with racial understanding may be defeated. You can't end wrong attitudes by kicking people in the teeth; you've even got to understand and forgive their errors—even let 'em ride for a while! If you take Robinson only for what he is—a great athletic star—you yourselves will be greater. Once you know that there are no such things as black or white home runs, you will eventually be able to believe there are no such things as black or white Americans."

When he paused, Rickey was astounded to see tears in the eyes of his guests. They were filled with hope.

"I don't have to tell you how to take care of this problem. You will know what should be done."

They knew and they did.

On April 10 of that same year the Dodgers were playing an exhibition game with Montreal in Ebbets Field at Brooklyn. On second base with the Royals, Robinson still did not know his fate, until, during the sixth-inning intermission, Rickey announced to the reporters that on the following day the first colored player in a big league would play against the Yankees as the permanent Dodgers' first baseman. That same afternoon Jackie Robinson crossed from the visiting team quarters to the Dodgers' locker room.

"I had prayed for that a long time," he told me. "When it happened it was like crossing the river Jordan!"

Right away those thirty-two leaders went to work. From pulpits of Negro churches pastors pleaded with the congregations:

"Don't spoil Jackie's chance."

From rostrums of secret fraternal lodges grand masters and potentates exhorted the brothers:

"Don't spoil Jackie's chance."

Even bartenders in gin mills lectured their customers:

"If you're drinking, stay away from the ball park. Give your tickets to somebody sober. Don't spoil Jackie's chance."

The word was going around that this was the time for a new attitude—yes, and a new dignity. Jackie Robinson had been picked, not to patronize or appease one separate segment of the community, but because he was a champion, a "must." The Dodgers had to have him, because he was a champion in his own right. "We must take that for granted now—if we look at *him* right, maybe people will begin to look at *us* right."

Let no one think it was easy. Some Jim Crow players in the league hated this new man's presence. One player comes sliding down to first base; the cruel spikes cut, deliberate and deep. Anger flames in Jackie; he is on fire to swing with his fists. But he can't do that. He promised Branch Rickey he wouldn't. So he swallows hard, as Rickey remembers him on that hot August day, under the benign and suffering portrait in his office. There is no brawl; the game goes on.

One Dodger asked Rickey to trade him to some other team where he could play with white men. That was in the early part of 1949. But before the World Series the player came back to the boss.

"Trade me if you insist, Mr. Rickey, but not for the reason I gave. I've come to think a lot of Jackie Robinson."

Walter White, great Negro leader, sat in a box during many a game. There was the time when Jackie hit a home run and tied the score.

"But," objected White, "no teammate went through the ritual, which is as much a part of baseball as the ball itself, of shaking hands with him when he crossed the plate. And, in the long walk between clubhouse and bench, while all the other players strolled in groups of two and three, Jackie walked alone."

In the locker room White demanded to know how things were going on the team, and Jackie answered:

"They're treating me all right. In fact, swell!"

Either Jackie or Rickey will tell you those players were doing the best they were capable of, at that point. And what must have been a thin hope that day was much nearer to a fact before season's end. It was not because of the acclaim Robinson had won, although there was much of that. The *Sporting News,* solid baseball authority, picked him as the "Rookie of the Year." *Time* magazine said that Jackie's season in the big league was the toughest first year any ballplayer has ever faced. More important, and solely because of Robinson, the estimated National League intake was nearly a quarter of a million dollars above normal.

What altered the attitudes of teammates was the proof Jackie Robinson had given that he was not only a great athlete but a real person. No white player ever had to withstand what he had taken without a protest.

When that exciting World Series was over, Jackie went back to California, still working hard between seasons. But the day was to come when he was to stand again before Branch Rickey's desk and talk the situation over. They knew the fight had only begun; old, unthinking animosities die hard. But they could see progress. That might be because Rickey, having done an audacious thing, did not condemn opponents as villains and morons. He took account of the backgrounds of prejudice; he sought to make progress peacefully, being harmless as a pigeon but careful also to be smart. Over the heads of the loudmouthed minority, he had reached the people, and by them Rickey's faith was justified. It was the same faith that had sustained the man with the trusting eyes, whose picture looked down upon the two of them—Rickey's long-time idol among men, Abraham Lincoln.

7

THE ROSE AND THE RING

*T*HE point which Albert Schweitzer drove home, over and over again, in his talks with me was that only in actual service, in personal hard work, can one best come to know that there is a God. It is the human tendency to absorb personal responsibility in the soulless operation of an organization, of a machine. But, more and more, the prophets of mechanics, the votaries of science are coming to realize that there is no God in their machinery. God still speaks only to the human being, made in His likeness. And it is still true that we must give ourselves; the gift without the giver is bare. And often it is tragically hard to give of ourselves.

The call for personal dedication often falls on deaf ears until we are overwhelmed in personal tragedy. Hildegarde Hawthorne, granddaughter of the great Nathaniel, once told me the story of her aunt Rose, one of the greatest of modern examples of how to know God by serving Him.

To the world that did not know her, Rose Hawthorne was an enigma in sacred and profane love. She was Nathaniel Hawthorne's youngest and most unmanageable child. Reared in comfort and culture, she left her home to share squalor and suffering with the penniless sick. Wife and mother, she ended her life as a nun, founder of the Servants of Relief for Incurable Cancer. She was a lacy valentine, transformed into a book of prayer.

As a child, little red-haired Rose was spoiled and head-strong and imperious. The family tried to trim their briery Rose with kindness. Once Nathaniel wrote her a small masterpiece of what the old Greeks called *apophasis*, the pretended denial of what one is saying:

Dear Little Rosebud:

I do hope you are a good little girl, and I am sure you never get into a passion, and never scream, and never scratch and strike your dear nurse or your dear sister, Una . . .

"I see how good Mama is," Rose answered, "but it don't make me good. The minute I have a chance, I am naughty." But, when older, she wrote to an aunt: "No one can tell how often and how severe my struggles are to be good . . . Do always think me a good girl till at last I *am* a good woman, without a narrow heart and mind."

There was nothing narrow about her. She loved gaiety and dancing, although she grew up in Concord, Massachusetts, among men and women whose interests were very thoughtful; companions whose like today could not be found. In summer she and her brother Julian bathed in Walden Pond with the Ralph Waldo Emersons. Neighbors and frequent household guests were Longfellow, Thoreau, and Oliver Wendell Holmes the elder; Louisa May Alcott, Whittier, and Agassiz.

While Rose was still very young, something happened to Nathaniel Hawthorne that was to leave an indelible mark.

He was then American consul in Liverpool, and he used to walk the slums of that old port and visit its almshouses, but always with anxiety that "I would catch some disease." One frosty morning, in the infirmary of an orphanage, a diseased little girl, face and hands covered with scabs, took a sudden, affectionate fancy to the American visitor. She beseeched him to lift her in his arms. Horror-struck, the sensitive Hawthorne nevertheless embraced the pitiful child, and afterward, writing as if it had happened to someone else, he called it: "an heroic act and effected more than he dreamed of toward his final salvation . . ."

As a child Rose wondered if God really expected refined people to clasp vile victims of life to their hearts. Did He want us to pick them up and kiss them? That hideous notion she cast out with a shiver.

Growing-up years were full of dances and roguish bantering with eligible young squires. Can we not see her at a costume ball, blithe, sprightly, and gay, as her sister Una described her:

Rose was Titania; had a very full, short dress of white Tarlatan, covered with silver spangles, and a pale blue and white sash draped over her shoulder, crossing her bosom and tying under her arms, and a crown of silver damascened with gold and covered with pearls and she carried a little gold wand tipped with flowers. . . .

The family expected great things of her talents for writing and painting and music. After Nathaniel Hawthorne died, Julian declared: "If there are, in any of the children, the remains of his genius, they will be found in Rose."

When the widow took her abroad to study art in Dresden, the one man in her life appeared. An old story will not down that Rose stole George Parsons Lathrop for herself just when Una and he were about to announce their engagement, and that the sacrifices of her later life were done in penance for that larceny. There was no truth to this idiotic gossip. Rose and George were nineteen; Una was seven years older and actually became engaged to Albert Webster, a young writer. Una herself was too ill to attend Rose's wedding, and her absence probably started all the talk.

Rose was in an ecstasy of romance. She had married the only man she ever loved, and the diamond ring and the gold band that so soon followed on her finger were to her symbols of lifelong joy. Yet Julian insisted at the time, and again fifty years later, that the marriage was a mistake and could never be set right. He was right, of course. But he never knew what happened to the golden ring and the diamond.

Although George lacked nothing in self-conceit, he had a social gift that made him popular. From a good family, he was handsome, debonair, and positive that he was to become the next great American author. Actually, he turned out to be a hard-working, fluent hack.

They were so young, and life held so many disappointments! Rose was a charming painter of little copies of famous pictures; never anything more than a skillful amateur. She wrote a few lovely poems; but her stories and articles, like her pictures, were not good enough. With what gifts they had, she and George made money, but were never hailed as great artists, as they had hoped to be. This fate Rose accepted calmly; George, with a feeling of injustice.

He became assistant editor of the *Atlantic Monthly*, held other literary jobs, and wrote endlessly—even making *The Scarlet Letter* into an opera. But his plaint was that he lived in the shadow of an overwhelming reputation which he could never overcome. "George Lathrop? Oh yes, Hawthorne's son-in-law!" Words he had heard too often!

A trifle over five years after the marriage their boy Francis was born, in November 1876, and early the following year Aunt Una died. She had been preparing to enter a Church of England convent at Windsor. Julian and his family were living in nearby Twickenham then, and now and again she visited them. During one of these visits she received the letter telling of the death of her fiancé. In the weeks that followed her hair turned gray; she returned to the convent and died suddenly.

Again the tongues of gossip wagged about Una and George, until he, in a burst of anger, gave a statement to the New York *Tribune*. Not only did he deny that he had been engaged to her, but he declared that his sister-in-law's mind was affected. As Rose's niece Hildegarde told me, those in the family knew that Una had never been crazy over George or anything else.

It was after this public outburst that George began to drink too much. Five years more of gradually increasing unhappiness for the young couple—and then the death of their little son. After that blow there never was much hope for them again as man and wife. After her boy's death, Rose arrived for a visit with Julian and his family, including little Hildegarde, in Jamaica, West Indies, where they had come from Sag Harbor. The tropics had never agreed with Hildegarde, and Rose begged the child's mother to let her take her niece home. During those next months the little girl came closer to her aunt Rose than ever before. On the homeward voyage Rose confided to the child her fear that she and her husband would have to part.

"There's no use denying that it gets more and more difficult for us to stay together. If we separate, I must find definite, useful work. I know you Swedenborgians believe in prayer as we do; my dearest Hildegarde, pray for me."

Yet for twelve years more George and Rose lived together, quarreling and making up, passing from one rift and reconciliation to another. Rose's grief seemed beyond solace, and George gradually became so violent and dangerous in his cups that at last his wife left him forever.

Alone, then, she came to her mysterious decision; not in any gush of feeling, but thoughtfully, arriving at an iron resolution in a quietude of grace.

Before the separation she had become a Roman Catholic, and George with her. Unhappily, their new-found faith had not kept them together. In solitary prayer now, she faced the fact that in all other pursuits she had failed. At forty-five she must begin some real work in the world, and she resolved on giving the rest of her life to helping the poor. From that moment on she decided "to live untrammeled by common sense."

"A fire," she declared, "was lighted in my heart." From this phrase her latest biographer, Theodore Maynard, took the title of his fine book, *A Fire Was Lighted*, to which I am greatly indebted.

But how would she help the poor? What made her course clear was the forsaken agony of her former seamstress, found dying in a basement on Blackwells Island, depot for the destitute sick. Thus Rose learned of the cruel state of penniless cancer victims. In that year of 1896 most people believed the disease to be "catching," like scarlet fever. Some families even put their own relatives out of the house, homeless victims in pain, wandering through back streets. At the same time Rose heard the story of Father Damien and the lepers of Molokai.

"I wish to serve the cancerous poor," she finally decided, "because they are avoided more than any other class of sufferers. I shall set my whole being to bringing consolation to them."

When Julian learned what she was doing, Hildegarde heard him say to her mother: "This is merely the supreme expression of her character. She has run to God this time, instead of to one of us."

Dark blue eyes filled with sober purpose, tawny dress and red hair making her a startling figure, she appeared one foggy morning in the front office of a clinic at Eighth Avenue and 106th Street.

"Teach me," she said to the doctors, "how to nurse the very worst cases." Like Nathaniel in Liverpool, she had to conquer horror; shuddering with an enormous pity, she resisted by sheer will power the impulse to run home. Three months she remained as an apprentice, learning what care and surcease could be given to victims who had the money to pay. And thus her purpose became clear and fixed—to bring the same peace and tenderness to those who had no money. From St. Vincent de Paul she took her motto: "I am for God and the poor."

Once she knew how to do the nursing, she set out to find a headquarters in the noisy, blustering slums of New York's Lower East Side. An overbearing young priest, wary of Lady Bountiful, advised her to go back where she came from and leave his vineyard to serious workers. Undismayed, and with little money to rely on, she promptly rented three tiny rooms over a bankrupt saloon. There was not an unbroken pane of glass in the whole blowzy, unkempt place where she would now live and work.

On her knees and all alone, she scrubbed the greasy walls and floors of the murky rooms till they were shining clean. She whose boudoir floor was once painted in pale rose now daubed the floor of her room for patients a vivid yellow as a kind of imitation sunshine.

Next day, wishing for more *sang-froid,* she sallied forth among curious and suspicious new neighbors. Denizens of those brawling lanes wondered what racket this redhead from society was up to. Blear-eyed, they watched her from windows and doorways, all so glum, so silent, that they frightened her.

"I was alarmed by the faces I saw, both of men and women," she later confessed contritely, "and feared that I might be robbed and even murdered if I lived among such characters."

Nor did matters improve when she stopped and explained how she had come there to give free nursing, to change bandages and dress wounds for women and children. That meant that she might be a plague carrier, full of deadly germs; even small boys of the tenements called names after her from the alleys. Presently, nevertheless, two people decided to seek her help.

A Jewish boy was her first case; an Irishwoman with crumbling face came second. When these two emerged into the street, newly tended and full of praise, the word began to spread. Within the next few weeks there came marching to the shaky old house at Number 1 Scammel Street a parade of the stricken: decrepit age and broken youth; hags and beldams and young slatterns, some with ravaged throats and making harsh guttural sounds; women and children of all ages, colors, religions—and all cursed with the same pollution. Not one was ever turned away.

Soon the red-haired stranger found friends and helpers. A doctor procured her official permits from the board of health and gave his services free as she might need them. A lawyer offered free legal aid. Volunteer nurses from uptown began to appear, although not many remained for long. Financial help came too, thanks to appeals she wrote for the readers' letter columns of the newspapers.

Hildegarde was one of those who volunteered to help, and later her younger sister Beatrix would come with her. Afternoons, Hildegarde would make bandages, help in cooking, and read aloud to a blind old man in his rented room across the street. The book was the latest literary sensation, a detective story about a brand-new hero called Sherlock Holmes. To the women residents in her aunt's spare room she read whatever they asked for.

Twice during the first year Rose nearly died of pneumonia; her own assistants nursed her back to life. There were a great many patients to be visited now; all too few could be received at the door for lack of room, and more space became essential. The second house was a two-story wooden shack, with dank basement and leaky roof, at 668 Water Street. There, with the flood of patients rising daily, fate interfered and the future of the work became assured.

One windy mid-December dusk there came up the dark stairs and into the lamplight a delicate stranger. Her name was Alice Huber, daughter of a Kentucky physician. An art instructor (her paintings hang today in many American chapels), Alice had no nursing experience. In uptown drawing rooms she had heard reports of what Rose was doing, and now, sitting beside Rose on an old green sofa, she volunteered a few hours every week. Her very first attempt to help a patient in the cheerless Water Street rooms was nearly her last: she blanched and nearly fainted.

But in Rose's diary, only three weeks later, you may read the simple entry: "Alice Huber has decided to give her life to the work."

The friendship of these two women, so utterly unlike, was never to falter, although in grueling partnership one lived to be seventy-five, the other eighty; Rose, ardent and confident, hurling herself, spendthrift, into every project; Alice, slow, careful, following up the grand rush with tidiness and order. Together they nursed their helpless, scrubbed the floors, and trained new volunteers. Before very long, in May 1899, they found much better quarters in an old-fashioned, comfortable house at Cherry Street, where they doubled the number of beds.

There were still many who tried to discourage Rose. One municipal official, even after seeing the work, bluntly predicted she would never get any thanks for it. She told him: "We plan to make this work so thoroughly and affection-ately gentle that even the poor can praise."

Which was like an echo of St. Vincent's dying warning to his helpers: "You must love the poor! That is the only hope you have that they will forgive you for the bread you give them."

One afternoon Alice was at the front door waiting when Rose trudged home from her saddest errand. George La-throp had died in Roosevelt Hospital before his wife, for all her frenzied hurrying, could reach his bedside. The widow came back to Cherry Street with her husband's prayer book in her hand.

The death of that unhappy man was to have two important effects. Until now there had been an aloofness in ecclesiastical circles about the work of the Servants of Relief for Incurable Cancer. But the crescendo of praise and thanks of grateful families could not be stilled, and there came a churchly change. Why should such work be done for women only? What about men sufferers? Why not a hospital to enlarge and stabilize the program? Indeed, why not a new order of nuns consecrated to this work alone, and with Rose Hawthorne Lathrop the first and founding Mother?

The idea of such a hospital had long been in Rose's mind; but she had fears about it, too, which made her stubborn and reluctant. She was afraid there would be a tendency to accept paying patients, and thus cut down space for the poor; against any such adulteration of her plan she was implacable. But a hospital under the control of a religious order would never lose its charity—and now, with George dead, there was no longer any impediment to taking the veil.

Thus the laughing, merry-hearted little Rose became Mother Alphonsa, founder of the Dominican Order of St. Rose of Lima, and Alice Huber became Sister Mary Rose. No sooner were they robed in white wool and dark wimples than they plunged into an audacious act of sanctified folly: they bought themselves a summer resort!

In their own deeply confident way, which was to go on spending almost the total of their funds—sure that Heaven would continue to supply more—they took a daring chance with their thousand dollars—all they possessed. The property, a former sixty-room hotel and nine parked and wooded acres, was on a hilltop in a Westchester village called Sherman Park (long since changed to Hawthorne). The price, in the spring of 1901, was twenty-eight thousand dollars. They could not resist. Those sylvan acres, with the spreading tops of shade trees, were like fairyland, although the wooden building was a firetrap. Immediate repairs would cost thousands of dollars; rebuilding, much more. Where was the money to come from?

Confident Rose and austere Alice, both untrammeled by common sense, handed over the whole thousand as a down payment, and took possession. Rosary Hill became a reality!

In spite of the shocked dismay of old settlers, learning that the hilltop had been turned into a lazaretto; of mortgages time and again about to be foreclosed; of ruined boilers and frightening coal bills; of a trouble and an obstacle and a scare for every dollar of their down payment; in spite of a thousand natural and unnatural shocks, these two women were able to keep the place open and going and to bring from the slums to their new branch all those who could stand or benefit by the change, there amid sweet air and old trees to lengthen lives and at the last to close the tired eyes in peace.

There is a story of how one banker came to the front door and told Rose there would be no more concessions; if she could not pay up the mortgage, he would take over.

"But," pleaded Mother Alphonsa, "we have been making a novena to get your money."

"What's a novena?"

"Nine days of prayer."

"When will you get through with it?"

"We finished the novena only an hour ago."

"Well, you didn't get the money. What will you do next?"

"Start another novena."

If that conversation really took place, Hildegarde told me, she could hear Aunt Rose chuckling about it, and see her kneeling in the chapel next morning, giving thanks for the legacy that actually came the same night, a few thousand dollars falling into their hands just when they needed it most—as always.

For thirty-one years Mother Alphonsa and Sister Mary Rose slaved for the doomed of the poor. Rich people, dying, left them a part of their wealth; contributions increased, and novice recruits volunteered in greater numbers and with firmer purpose. Most of their money still came in gifts from little people; as always Rose relied upon what she called in her magazine, *Christ's Poor*, "the daily mercy of the public." Mark Twain predicted for her work: "Its prosperity will be permanent, since it has its endowment banked where it cannot fail until pity fails in the hearts of men."

Before many years the order and its labors were to spread. Today there are hospitals in Atlanta, Fall River, Philadelphia, St. Paul; and, in New York City, the modern St. Rose's Home, with its one hundred beds, at 71 Jackson Street. There would be many more—one in every community, no doubt—except for the lack of women to do such forbidding work, sisters with the resolution and grace to follow in the footsteps of Mother Alphonsa and Sister Mary Rose. In one recent year their hospitals cared for 1600 patients, of which 939 were Catholic, 636 Protestant, and a scattering of Jews and Orthodox Greek; nearly 200 were Negroes.

Rabbis and Protestant ministers come, with the priests, each to console his own, on Rosary Hill; for there is still no distinction of creed or color in this democracy of mercy.

"Mother," a visitor once said to Rose, "I wouldn't do what you are doing for a million dollars."

"Neither would I," was the gaily chuckled answer. Long before, she had written: "From the first the charity has been regarded as a religious work, since no inducement outside of religion would be sufficient."

All through the years Mother Alphonsa slept in a bare room, with only a little bed and two stools, a candle and a crucifix. Surely it would seem that the past were washed from her heart. But she would, I think, not have put it so. Instead, she might have said that the past had been but steps along the road of life, the path chosen of God; to Him she offered it all up—her failure, her folly, her griefs, her joys, her deep, undying devotion to her husband. Never once in all the busy years after George's death did she sign her name other than as Mother Alphonsa Lathrop.

When he was eighty years old, Julian went to see her at the celebration of her seventy-fifth birthday, which was to be her last. But George was never mentioned; on the point of that marriage brother and sister still could not entirely agree, even in their last days on earth.

I believe that July 8, 1926, was the happiest day of Rose's life. Permission had been received some time before to start the building of a handsome new fireproof hospital on a site chosen by Rose, high on the hill. After the cornerstone, signal of the building's birth, had been blessed, Rose walked with the archbishop, showing him the views and explaining how the hospital was to look like one of the old California missions.

"I can almost see it." She smiled at him. "When I close my eyes I feel it, like a living thing, in my heart."

Guests remarked on the lovely face of the Mother Superior, the look of light it had that day. Sister Mary Rose, who had come from the hospital in New York City, said:

"I've seen her meet many a bitter difficulty with a smile, but I've never seen it so—well, shining—as now."

But for all its happiness, the day had been tiring, and soon Mother Alphonsa went to her room. The two who had toiled so long together parted in the corridor.

"Tomorrow all the workmen will start; it won't be long before it is finished," said Sister Mary Rose.

"Tomorrow, the real beginning!" whispered Mother Alphonsa, and closed her door.

Next morning, when she failed to come down to breakfast, one of the young sisters ran up to call her. But Mother Alphonsa, Nathaniel Hawthorne's "little Rosebud," had gone to join him. She had finished her work in this world.

If you visit Rosary Hill, you will find there certain symbols of the sacred and the profane love that Rose Hawthorne wove into a miracle of pity and service: Near the altar lies George's prayer book. And on the little hand of a statue of the Christ Child gleam her engagement and her wedding rings.

Rose Hawthorne knew there was a God. She knew Him intimately, because for His sake she gave everything.

8

GOD IN THE FACTORIES

*I*T IS a common fallacy of the time that there is no room for God in a practical and realistic workaday world. That, of course, is where a knowledge of God is needed most of all; it is where miracles occur, not only in the lives of individuals, but also in labor relations, in prosperity, in the quality and security of society. Let no one make us believe that, in these days of specialization, it is intellect's job alone to solve our problems. Faith is not to be consigned to the back yard, like a charming child who knows nothing of the ways of the world.

Where is faith's place? In the home, yes—and in the heart. But also in the legislatures, the schools, the union meetings, the offices, the factories. We cannot, if we are true Christians, be souls devoted to God at home and then forget about Him when we step out the front door. Faith is not something to be thought about in off hours, along with movies, radio, and television.

In education, office, factory, government we need the ever-steady beacon of Christ's teaching. Tony Montiero, for example, has proved what the knowledge of God can do in the factory.

The story, as Tony told it to me, began one busy Monday in the midst of the war.

The president of the Barnett Foundry and Machine Company had given strict orders not to be disturbed. Alone in his private office at the Irvington, New Jersey, plant, he looked up from a tangle of figures to see his secretary apologizing in the doorway.

"There's a man outside, Mr. Edinger, who won't go away. He says his business is just as important as winning the war."

"Screwball?"

"Polite—but awful determined."

"Send him in," sighed H. L. Edinger.

Presently, on the other side of the desk, there loomed a man of wrestler build, in blue work pants, asbestos leggings and leather jacket. Nervously his mighty hands were fisting and opening, and there was an ecstatic gleam in the rolling black eyes.

"Boss, my name is Tony Montiero. I've just read a notice on the bulletin board. It says we've got to work every other Sunday from now on."

"Only because of the extreme urgency of increased production. The Army——"

"Do you realize that if men have only two Sundays off a month, they'll spend them in bed resting up?"

"So what?"

"So they'll never go to church!" exploded Tony.

The bewildered Edinger gasped. He demanded to know why Tony cared about that, and then the workman's moonlike face flushed to the roots of disorderly black curls.

"By day," he confessed, "I am a patternmaker in molders' alley here. But at night I study at Bloomfield

Theological Seminary. Someday I'm going to be a regular ordained minister."

"Well," said Edinger heartily, "I'm glad to know that, of course. Just the same, there's nothing I can do——"

"There is something we *both* can do," cut in Tony earnestly, "if you'll only give it a chance."

Later that March afternoon in 1942 a new notice was tacked on the Barnett bulletin board:

"Tony Montiero will hold nonsectarian services next Sunday, 12:20 noon, in the machine shop."

For the rest of the week only one question buzzed, high and low, through the factory:

"What's Montiero doing it for?"

The enigma was troubling not only the eight hundred workers but also Mr. Edinger's associates in management. Each group feared the factory chapel service was a trick of the other side; doubts and rumors seethed in the plant, which is located in the midst of the "tough" New York and New Jersey industrial area, where for years labor troubles had been increasing. But now the Portuguese molder and seminarian, having just nailed up his notice, was bringing into industry a new thing.

Tony's first altar was a sludge box, his first cross fashioned of broomsticks nailed together, his first flag borrowed from a veteran's grave. The pews were planks laid over crosstrees, and there were not nearly enough of them for the battalions of the curious who trooped in at the appointed hour.

From that first service on, crowds have always come to his meetings; union men, bookkeepers and supervisors; grizzled faces cheek by jowl with smooth young ones as yet unmarked by a wrinkle; bosses and local union officials, in the midst of brattle and uproar, surrounded with forges and cranes and hissing lights, furnaces and boiling metal.

In steamy heat they squatted on the floor, half expecting a gimmick in the plan, all ready to denounce a fraud on the human heart, if necessary. But they joined in the Lord's Prayer, in singing "The Old Rugged Cross," and in listening to the husky young giant read from the Testaments, Old and New. Then he preached to them on simple patterns of human behavior until a whistle blew and the first service was over.

Today the Reverend Anthony Montiero is an ordained, official home missionary of the Presbyterian Church. He has congregations in eleven factories, all of different ownership and management, and all distinguished for constantly improving working conditions, achieved without hate, struggle, or strikes.

Every Sunday, in some pulpit in New Jersey, you can find Dr. Montiero, very impressive in canonical gown with black velvet collar. But on weekdays you will find the same old big-fisted molder and patternmaker ministering to his factory flocks in the place where they work, offering his shopmates serenity of conscience, well-being of body, mind and soul; all this and Heaven too, as free gifts. Tony never takes up a collection, and management gives him nothing; his only pay is a salary from the Presbyterian Synod. There have been other industrial chaplains hired by bosses to preach to men, but Tony Montiero is the first to found real congregations in factories, free from bosses or labor control.

In the concrete acreage of industrial plants, far more than in church pulpits, Tony feels exuberantly at home. Most of his early life was spent at workbenches; he had been a factory hand for eighteen years before he finished night high school and began to study theology and Bible history.

George Wendell Jung, vice-president of eighty-year-old Bloomfield College, compares their pioneer industrial dominie to circuit pastors of colonial days, equestrian evangelists who rode through blizzard and scorching heat to preach the Gospel in remote hamlets. Montiero rides to the concentration of vast factory populations, finding there a loss of faith greater than ever was known in the old wilderness. Owning neither horse nor auto, he is constantly getting around by bus and trolley.

Often his advice to parishioners seems inspired, as in the case of little Joe, the "incurable" gambler.

Joe, with his sandy hair and soulful blue eyes, was a four-foot, nine-inch miniature, with a tiny wife, a tiny boy and girl, and apparently very little common sense. Every payday he would scurry from the factory to shoot craps in the back of a filling station. He was always ready to bet on anything from a Kentucky Derby long shot to a blue-toothed housefly in a crawl up a saloon windowpane. So Joe often arrived home with empty pockets. "I'm incurable," he would boast; "like a kleptomaniac or an alcoholic."

"If you can't stop gambling, neither can your family stop eating," was the decision of his miniature golden-haired wife. Taking the children, she went home to mother in a faraway state. But Joe only felt sorry for himself, and brooded so miserably over his sharp-bladed machinery that before he knew what was happening one morning it had nearly chopped off his right arm.

When Tony Montiero called at the hospital, he received a surly greeting: "Go on! Tell me this is the judgment of

God. Because I shoot a little craps, He tries to take away my wife and my right hand."

"No," Tony demurred, "that isn't what happened. You can go back to your old job. And you still have a wonderful future if you quit gambling!"

"Not me!" stormed the amputee. "I'll show you! I can shake dice with my good hand."

But now he had to cut his risks in half, because a court order dispatched half of his wages to his wife. Big-fisted Tony grabbed the little fellow by the collar one high noon and told him off:

"If you can cut down 50 per cent on craps because you have to, you can do 100 per cent, if you want to. You're a very lonesome man. Better come with me."

He led the gambler to a distant lunch wagon where he had arranged for the wife and children to be waiting. When he saw them, Joe wiped his eyes; he couldn't speak.

"We'll come back if you'll only just give up gambling," pleaded the wife. "We all love you."

"How can I ever stop?" argued little Joe miserably. "I've tried before. It just overpowers me."

"You don't have to stop," Tony interposed amazingly. And waggling a pudgy forefinger at Joe, he declared:

"The only thing that matters with you is what you gamble *for*. What're your stakes? Joe, you know as well as I do, you are a tinhorn sport; a cheapskate, betting your own home, your own wife, your own kids—all you've got in the world against a few lousy dollars. Why don't you put your bank roll on the real sweepstakes? Lay your dough on your kids! Right on the nose! Bet that the cost of sending that bright-faced son through college will pay off in his future, so you'll be proud of him. And that the right clothes and shoes and education will lead his sister to a fine future too. You'll still be gambling—but you'll be out of the honky-tonk class, and playing for big stakes!"

There is magic in a changed attitude. That bawling out was what Joe needed. Today he will tell you with a rueful grin that he has kidded himself into actually feeling a thrill when he banks his savings every Saturday; he has not quit the game at all, he is playing for the jackpot.

Tony is bluntly frank, not only in private talks, but in his sermons.

"What's to prevent us union men from taking all the profits away from the boss once we're strong enough? What use is fair play anyway? The answer is deep in your heart and mine: we simply don't any of us live by bread alone. We are not just economic units; we are children of God, all brothers of one family—and we must do as we would be done by."

To a group who argued that Communism was Christianity made practical, he retorted:

"It just ain't so! You have to make a choice. It's Christ *or* Communism. Don't believe the dopey thinkers that tell you different. If you want Communism, you can't keep Christ, because Karl Marx, the founder of Communism, said this: 'The democratic concept of man is false because it is Christian. The democratic system held that . . . each man is a sovereign being. This is the delusion, the dream, of Christianity.' "

And then, husky voice soaring, he rushed on:

"Communism wants to bring all men down to one level by class warfare. That's by hate. Christianity will lift all men to a higher level by brotherhood. That's by love. You can decide for yourselves whether you prefer to live by hate or by love."

His sermons are reproduced in the mimeographed *Industrial Chaplain News,* which is syndicated through all eleven plants, with news items, birthday greetings to hundreds of workmen, and jokes and chitchat gathered by the shop dominie. Tucked into pay envelopes are trenchant excerpts on alcoholism, gambling, and venereal disease.

If men are ill, at home or in hospital, or if they are in the jailhouse, Tony visits them. He calls on feeble shut-in parents, sick wives and children, jesting and praying his way around a broad area of heartache. Because most of these factory men have long been unchurched, and many never belonged to any congregation, the friendly interest Tony displays comes as a stunning surprise, a tonic to morale. Some of them have scoffed at Bible reading, but they never jeer at the words of Jesus read at a sickbed. The thousands of calls Tony has made in Verona Sanitarium and the Elizabeth General Hospital, and other thousands in homes, have given religious faith an intense new meaning to hosts of the indifferent.

He has coaxed Jews back to synagogues, Protestants to prayer meeting, Catholics to Mass. He has given away hundreds of Bibles. He has converted more than a score of Communists to Christianity.

That one church is as good as another, the author does not maintain, and the story of Tony is not told to prepare a favorable reception for that error. And it will be pointed out that the combined religious services contradict dogma. But if Tony were asked about the basis of his work he would reply that what he is trying to do is to get all men to follow their highest convictions. And all men who do that are members of Christ's Church in desire.

Since he began his ministry not a single major strike has occurred in the eleven plants where he holds services. In 1948 there was not a single disturbance between labor and management, except one inconsequential flurry that ended in less than twenty-four hours. He can call every one of his four thousand parishioners by name. Nor is it only workmen that he touches with the vision and hope of a better life. Brass hats of management have also gone back to their churches, thanks solely to the example of Tony's life.

One night a young man lay intoxicated and helpless in the middle of a New Jersey street. From the sidewalk a crowd of spectators stood gawking at the poor devil's futile attempts to get to his feet, and listening to the sulphurous oaths with which he cursed his own condition. Suddenly a man jumped from a passing bus, beckoned a taxi, and then lifted the young sot from the gutter. In husky voice he crooned to the blaspheming drunkard:

"Never mind, boy! I'll fix that cut on your face. I'll give you a bath. I'll get you out of this."

A cheer went up from the do-nothing crowd as Tony drove off with his burden. Finding him was sheer coincidence; not until later did the chaplain discover that the young man was the wastrel heir of a wealthy father. The father never knew how Tony led his young problem to Alcoholics Anonymous so that eventually he rid himself of his obsession for liquor.

A different sort altogether was Jerry, who pasted on the wall behind his bench a voluptuous pin-up strip-teaser.

"What is that thing?" asked Tony in sepulchral voice.

"That's art, Padre. You don't understand art. So let's not talk about it."

"That picture is unsettling to me as a mere spectator. To you, as a workman at a dangerous machine, it's a menace."

"It stimulates me to greater efforts to win the war," the workman teased with a Simple Simon grin.

A week later Tony came back with a brief case.

"You said I didn't know anything about art. What about this?"

Evidently Tony had called at Jerry's home, for he now produced a lovely picture of the workman's wife.

"And," the pastor added, "since I hear your first child is well on the way, I also brought you another work of art."

It was a colored print of Raphael's Mother and Child in the Chair. Without a word Tony affixed both pictures to the wall and stood back to admire. Swearing aloud, Jerry tore down his brazen hussy and cast her away.

"You know, Padre," he said, "I'll tell you now what I swore I wouldn't. Yesterday I nearly did get hurt because I got to thinking about that picture. You're right! But just the same, I don't mind telling you, life is hell."

He felt differently when Tony baptized the baby son. "I guess," Jerry said, "religion really amounts to a man growing up!"

There is no question that Montiero is an ever-present help in the private lives of his people. He has also fostered within his industrial parishes better employer-employee relations. After six years of the experiment Bloomfield College has instituted a course in Industrial Chaplaining, "to prepare minister and Christian lay worker, missionaries, and labor leaders of the future." Of course Tony is the first professor of the undertaking. Three times a week he instructs young students from his experiences. Industrial chaplains of the future, he believes, must come from the ranks of workers, as he did; he still carries his union cards as a member in good standing of Local No. 40, I.M. and F.W.U. of N.A.

It was years ago now that labor and management in the Barnett plant, where it all started, were asking the same suspicious question: "What's Montiero doing it for?"

As a sample answer, take this letter from Kenneth W. Wantz, vice-president of the Atlas Foundry Company:

When absenteeism had reached an unheard-of peak, and tension was at the utmost, we heard of the excellent work Rev. Montiero was doing for industry. We decided to try his plan in our plant. It was a tremendous morale builder and seemed to break the tension which existed between the workingmen and management. We have continued and will continue to have these services.

Union officials put it differently:

An open letter to our Industrial Chaplain.
My Dear Rev. A. A. Montiero & Brother:

There are moments in a man's life when he wishes to express his views and sentiments, shall I say to a swell guy, who is doing a swell job.

In following the footsteps of Jesus, you have in your humble way, visited the sick, the lame, and the blind, you have never stinted yourself as to where these sick brothers lived, you reached down into your pockets, paid your own transportation, whether by train, trolley or bus, distance was no object to you, so as you got there to visit the brothers, and to wish them a speedy recovery.

Not only did you visit the sick, you took it on your own shoulders to investigate their financial situation and if you found they needed any help, you took it up with the proper authorities and saw to it that that certain family got that help. We know you did just that, and without any fanfare, and the Local appreciates it. We also wish you and the Family the best of health, and may God give you that strength to carry on your noble work.

Fraternally yours.

The letter was signed by the correspondent reporter, president, vice-president, and the financial secretary-treasurer.

And finally, from neither union nor employer, but from a group of workmen, came this message:

"You bring us closer to God and to our fellow human beings."

And that, of course, is what Tony is doing it for!

9

THE WAY YOU LOOK AT IT

 *T*o KNOW God is to try to look at things as He would look at them. There is no greater secret of happiness than to do just that. And I have found scientific confirmation for this mystical practice from one of the great neurologists of today, a man with the gift of curing heartaches. I call him Dr. Edwin.

He was a psychologist who worshiped God, a psychiatrist who belonged to a church, an analyst who came to know and understand confusion and despair, not only in a clinic but first in his own breast. For many years he was a potent and inspiring force in a great neurological institute. Now, in frail old age and retirement, he is called by doctors and nurses their saint emeritus.

Nervous wrecks he salvaged, neurotics whom he led into new patterns and directions, cowards he heartened, and the persecuted from whom he banished delusions—all had the benefit of modern hospital techniques. But not from Dr. Edwin. He refused to stir up the muddy wells of memory and the unconscious; he let others practice analysis and group therapy and shock treatments.

His own way was to talk to patients like a Dutch uncle;

to tell them parables of a psychologist, and to point up the meaning with a rugged and healthy bluntness.

"You," he often told them, "are the sole cause of your condition—and only you can cure yourself."

A fribbling woman came in one day, full of foolish complaints: "I am completely worn out; I just can't stand another hour of it, Doctor; everything—including my husband, my children, and the dog—is getting on my nerves."

She would have gone away perfectly satisfied with a prescription for barbiturate sleeping pills and perhaps a suggested South American cruise. But Dr. Edwin seldom gave prescriptions like that; no professional flummery and humbug from him! Instead, he told her about a woman in a fashionable Boston hotel who called the manager and said:

"I am ready to scream. I am dizzy and faint; my whole body is trembling, and I see black spots in front of my eyes. Somebody in the next room has been banging on a piano the whole day long. If you don't have it stopped at once, I'm going to collapse and be sent to a hospital, and you will be responsible!"

"Ah, madam," groaned the clerk. "I wish I could help you, but I just don't dare. You see, he is rehearsing for his concert tonight in Symphony Hall—it's Paderewski!"

"Really?" quavered the complainant. "Oh, that's different!"

The very next minute she was on the telephone, inviting friends to come right over and listen with her. Soon the pianist had a rapt audience in the next room, and the hostess had miraculously recovered from her attack of nerves.

"Nothing at all had changed," said Dr. Edwin, "except,

of course, her own attitude." And nothing, he adds, is so important as the way a person chooses—the way he *decides* —to look at things. That is what some psychologists call an evaluative attitude, which simply means the way in which one elects to size up a situation. The whole character of a man consists of the sum total of such attitudes.

There is an intimate relationship between such mental attitudes and physical illness.

"More diseases are caused by a malevolent, 'bad wishing' point of view than by germs," Dr. Edwin would tell his patients. "Our bodies have a natural resistance to microbes, but the defense can be broken down by grudges, resentments, and hates—*even little ones,* if we have enough of them. For example, your brooding over a slight—real or fancied—could open a defensive door and let in the flu, and then you are laid up for a week solely because you have looked at a thing the wrong way, the uncharitable way.

"Time is showing that Hippocrates was right, when, four hundred years before Christ, he declared that anger and fear breed a poison in the blood. A perfectly healthy person can be overcome by vengeful ideas and eventually be crippled by arthritis or rheumatism for the rest of his life."

And then Dr. Edwin told me about a woman brought into a great New York hospital to be operated on for a duodenal ulcer. With a diabolical gleam of triumph in her eye, she told the surgeon:

"My husband knew I wanted a fur coat for Christmas. He said he couldn't afford it. Mind you, the miserable thing only cost $650. Now this operation is going to set the old miser back $1500."

She seemed to have no idea what her resentful attitude was costing *her*. Yet the ulcer was a physical outcome of emotional storms—the infernal cause of many ulcers.

Common sense, the knack of seeing things as they are, is our best protection. There is an old prayer which runs: "God give me the strength to change the wrongs I can change, and to accept the wrongs I cannot change, and the wisdom to know the difference."

In an old-time rune, Isaac Watts put it another way:

"What's amiss I'll strive to mend, and endure what can't be mended."

With such a spirit of good will a man can do more than merely avoid the penalties of malevolence; he can actively help himself to get ahead in life. Success can be hastened by the right attitude, which might be defined as deciding to make the best of the worst. Far from being a namby-pamby, inane, or weakly insipid course, this is hard, practical psychological technique; it takes a man, not a jellyfish, to live victoriously.

Thus resolved, however, we often discover how things can be mended, when no solution seems possible. A lovely young violinist from a middle-western town is the heroine of one of Dr. Edwin's favorite parables from real life. At an early age Frances toured Nebraska, Iowa, and other states with her own chamber-music quartet. Suddenly her widower father was paralyzed; she gave up her tours to stay at home, to nurse and comfort him. By the time he died, two years later, the savings were almost exhausted; with what was left, Frances came to New York. But she had no fear. A good violinist, she would surely find work on the radio. Only after months did she come to realize how many thousands of other young violinists had the same idea. That was when Frances had a heart-to-heart talk with the memory of her father.

"You always told me not to quail before facts, Daddy, but to look them in the eye."

So, with her remaining two hundred dollars, Frances put her musical training aside and entered business college to learn the stenographic and secretarial mysteries. Graduated near the top of her class, she still could not find work. The depression was dismal then; there were too many secretaries. Again she consulted her father's wisdom. "Look at the difficulty," he used to say, "and tell yourself what has to be done."

The following Sunday this ad appeared in a New York classified column:

I can't get a job without experience. And I can't get experience without a job. That is why I will work four weeks for you without pay—and then leave you. You have no obligation whatever. And I'm good!

She received more than a thousand replies, picked three of the best, and made her arrangements with them. At the end of the first week in her first job she was handed an envelope containing thirty-five dollars. After four weeks she was offered a permanent job but refused it; she wanted only a letter of recommendation. At the end of three months she had worked for three reputable firms; she had been paid a full salary every week, and when, right afterward, she applied to a well-known lawyer for a permanent job she was able to display those iridescent testimonials. The sequel was that the late Colonel Louis McHenry Howe, confidential aide to President Roosevelt, liked her so much that she eventually left the lawyer's office to take a secretarial post in the White House!

And there was Rosa, a girl who wanted to draw and paint. Yes, experts told her, she had talent, but she was too poor to pay for tutoring in the ateliers, or to pay a model to pose for her at home.

"I must find a model who will stand still without fee," Rosa told herself—and she found not one but a hundred in the tethered farm horses of Parisian marketmen. Because she made the best of what she had, Rosa Bonheur gained the fame of the world as a painter of animal life.

To acquire that right point of view—and cleave to it— is never easy. Somehow we tend to look at the wrong thing in the wrong way. To prove this Dr. Edwin once conducted a remarkable experiment. The head of a factory, frightened at a slump in company business, had asked the psychologist to make a talk to a discouraged sales force. Dr. Edwin appeared on the platform carrying a large sheet of white cardboard. Holding it high, he singled out the sales manager sitting in the front row, and asked:

"Would you mind telling us what you see?"

The manager contemplated the exhibit with shrewd eyes and finally answered:

"In the lower left-hand corner I see a round black dot."

Man after man in the audience made a similar answer. They were all positive they saw the little black dot. And then Dr. Edwin said:

"What you saw is what you chose to see. Except for that one unimportant little dot, this sheet is blank. There is enough white space there for Shakespeare to write Hamlet's soliloquy, Lincoln his Gettysburg speech, Moses the Ten Commandments. More, there is space there to compose an advertisement that might galvanize your sales. But you must decide whether to see a fly speck or an opportunity."

With Dr. Edwin the point of view is not merely mental acrobatics, it is a soul's conversion. It means never bewailing what is lost, but using what is left. That is a spiritual attitude, hardly arrived at; not merely cheerless submission to the inevitable, but full surrender. Between the two words, submission and surrender, Dr. Edwin sees the difference between torment and peace, between madness and sanity. The man who merely submits has a gleam in his eye, a whisper in the brain which says: "My time will come. I'll get even for this. You'll see."

That is also the mental state of most demented persons. "If they cannot change that attitude, they seldom if ever get well," Dr. Edwin told me. "If they can—if they *surrender*—they generally do get well. For surrender implies a dropping of the fight, expurging the past, blotting it out—the willingness to forgive and to co-operate, to start over again on a foundation of good will. Job feels the rod, yet still blesses God. No external circumstances can bring about that conversion. It must happen inside the individual. He must decide how he is going to look at his own case."

The tragedy is that many more persons are mentally sick outside of asylums than in them—and for the same shoddy causes: "He told somebody that I was a fool at the bridge table. He can't do that to *me*. I don't have to take that from *anybody!*"

Resentment grows by feeding on injured feelings. In

the grip of hostility I can lie awake nights making out a plausible case against my enemy; I concoct new suspicions, read mean motives into another's word or deed; I toss from side to side, composing an angry letter. Such a state of mind is a robber of sleep, a nightmare-maker; it rouses me without appetite, sends me to work with a chip on my shoulder, and goads me on to a quarrel.

All this because I *chose* to be offended; because I *decided* I was hurt. Had I chosen to smile it off, to make nothing of it, everything would be different.

"If you think you have been badly treated by your family or dearest friend," Dr. Edwin tells such disheartened people, "remember blind Milton's daughters. They were too lazy to read to him, sold his books to buy ribbons for themselves, and told him the library had been robbed. Milton learned the truth, but it did not prevent him from writing *Paradise Lost*."

One word of caution from Dr. Edwin: We seldom can see the generous point of view when we are offended; often we cannot even want to see it. Nothing decisive should ever be done in anger; the people who wind up in asylums are more often than not those who came to conclusions in passion rather than in thought; who have allowed emotion to usurp the authority of good sense.

I think his favorite parable is the true story of Henry Fawcett, who, in his twenties, went on a hunting trip with his father. By a tragic mishap Henry became the target of his father's rifle; he was shot in both eyes. Blinded for life.

It might be argued that an ambitious man like Henry Fawcett was entitled to feel the deeps of bitterness and despair. That was how it did seem to him at first; the only thing that saved him from final despondency was one stupendous fact: he deeply loved his father. Grief over the accident could break his father's life, and in order to spare him Henry pretended to a cheerfulness that was wholly false; he put on an appearance of gallantry that filled everyone with admiration. Here, indeed, was a man who chose how to react.

Odd to report, the pretended became the real. It was as if, by an act of will, he had exorcised an evil spirit, driving it out of himself. Henry Fawcett was elected to Parliament; later, at Gladstone's request, he became postmaster general; he brought about great improvements in the English postal and telegraph systems. Deliberately altering his attitude, he lived a useful career and found a good life for himself, mastering fate. Yet he *could* have chosen a lifetime of bitterness and misery.

Most of us do not have to face high tragedy; we are more likely to have a ceaseless round of little troubles, aggravations, anxieties, and affronts. When these pile up we sometimes decide to have an old-fashioned nervous breakdown, a kind of middle-aged tantrum. To such harassed patients, Dr. Edwin, old savant of the soul, would sometimes tell a different parable:

"I had a curious experience today. I went into a large hall and saw two men fighting. One yelled to the other: 'Hit me harder! Hit me a lot harder! What do you think I'm paying you for?'

"It seemed very odd until I learned that the complaining boxer was the contender in a championship bout; this was a hired sparring partner who wasn't punching as hard as the defending champ would be sure to hit. Because he wanted to be champion, the contender pleaded for punishment. There are very few spiritual champions, but we can all be contenders. As athletes of the soul, we can accept the trials that make us strong."

10

LOST ENCHANTMENT

*T*O KNOW God, and then to lose Him, not to know Him any more—that is the kind of lost enchantment that plagues our life.

Not in utter nakedness are we born into the world. As the poet has told us, we come, trailing clouds of glory, from God, who is our home. But soon the glory passes. Why is it that so many of us begin as dreamers and grow up to be cynics? Why do our young men and women scoff at God and religion as old-fashioned stuff?

Troubled by that solemn and familiar fact, my young friends themselves cross-examine me:

"Are we ourselves to blame? There was a time when we felt ready to die for our ideals, for they seemed so real and vital. Now we say they are impractical in a modern age. Why is it so hard to hold onto all the beautiful notions we used to believe in?"

Here, standing at the open doors of life, is a college girl. There is a lodestar in her eyes; she is not afraid of the future, for she means never to strike her flag to the spirit of lies and greed and shoddy compromise. Yet what a change slowly creeps over her! Five years later she sits at table with her husband and his friends and endures, without uttering a protest, the stealthy pawing of an old man she has just met. Why? Because he is an out-of-town buyer and can favor her husband with a juicy contract, and then they can buy that new car.

Who can forget George Eliot's story of the artist who spent a lifetime painting a picture of the Last Supper? His model for the Nazarene was the most beautiful and innocent youth in Florence. Years later, for the last figure on the canvas, the artist hired a beggar from the streets. In the doorway the beggar began to weep, for he, who had once been chosen as the perfect model for the Master, was now to pose as the living image of Judas.

When I was young the tale seemed only melodrama to me, but now I know that into our hearts come invisible changes just as shocking. Having once served the highest and best, we sell out for the cheapest prizes of life.

But I am also convinced that youth never disenchants itself. The boy does not learn atheism on the ball field. But the day may come when he enters a philosophy class and hears his new professor say: "If anyone here believes in religion, he will no longer believe in it by the time he finishes this course."

Disillusion comes from those we trust; it is a disease youth catches from age. In our middle-aged treason we turn with superior smiles and speak a malediction: "You have beautiful ideas, but they are not practical. In this life it's every man for himself. Just wait and see."

Up the street lives a woman who, like Chaucer's Wife of Bath, has had five church-door husbands, besides other company in her youth. She proclaims herself modern, liberated from foolish old taboos. Yet years ago, when she first fell in love with the boy around the corner, there was no brazen calculation in her glances. Because affection swept her into currents and depths seemingly beyond understanding, she loved her way trustingly into catastrophe. Then her young knight, with whom she had expected to live happily ever after, ran away, never to see her again.

That was disillusioning enough, but even more so was the sympathy and counsel of her friends. The death of love? Forget that corny stuff! Just learn hereafter to hold out, dearie; not for idealistic reasons, but simply to protect yourself financially. Make sure you are getting the cash for value received. So our young girl comes to a hardened calculation; she marries, makes a cash settlement, divorces and marries again; and these calculated faults are far more sordid than her first offense, which she committed in generous passion and trust.

What that girl needed, in the beginning, no doubt, was some frank and warning sex instruction. But would such lessons have kept her dreams alive? The problem, I fear, lies deeper. For today, in spite of social-hygiene classes, the ideas of a young girl are prone to be yanked out of proportion.

I believe in *complete* instruction—and "complete" belongs in italics, because it includes beauty and love. Today, in and out of schools, you may be as frank as you like about the mechanics and athletics of sex, but it is most improper to talk about it in terms of spirituality; that is the modern indelicacy.

What a girl is likely to be shown in class is a picture of physical love quite as false and incomplete as the old-time sentimental chromo of birds and bees and flowers. The new picture is denuded of beauty, diagrammatic, an X-ray negative—all blur and bones, like something from the grave.

This at a time when a girl is in the prime of her dreams. If she is lovingly taught, her reason can perceive the intellectual logic of chastity. But others argue that she has a right to experiment and make sure that she is finding her proper mate. This spurious indoctrination has persuaded many that the ideal of chastity is false. Why not teach the indisputable fact that often husbands and wives have to learn together?

Materialists who would assure this girl that sex is an animal instinct to be gratified and forgotten do not understand animals—and, in fact, basely libel them. For these creatures of instinct faithfully obey the laws which govern them, fulfilling their nature. Birds do not merely enjoy the pleasure of sex; they laboriously build their nests, the mother sits and hatches while the father fetches her food, and they both feed their young and teach them to be self-reliant. All this they do by their instincts, which are almost infallibly right. Man is the only creature who lives mainly by choice. He has free will, and his instincts are notoriously fallible. From birth to death man is always in a dangerous position, because, 99 times out of 100, he must make correct choices in his free-will decisions, if he is to be as right as the animals.

How then can man—a young girl, you, I, or anyone under Heaven—hope to be right that often? Only by relying on the moral training of the race, those ideals and beliefs we admired in our youth. There is more than rhetoric to our codes of conduct; behind them range thousands of years of bitter experience.

Often a young man begins with bold courage, like St. Paul, resolved to try all things and hold fast to that which is good; he passionately believes in his basic ideals: honor and courage and fair play and incorruptibility. Nothing, he thinks, shall ever bribe him; he will remain unpurchasable, intending, with Kant, to preserve "that divine man within us."

But tomorrow is full of sinister surprises. He learns that there is in town a criminal lawyer who, for a quarter of a century, by filthy little tricks and chicaneries, has defended thieves and gangster clients and set them free for fresh pillage. Now, with silver around his temples, as in his pockets, this lawyer becomes a candidate for judge. Good citizens should rise up and defeat such a man, but our young idealist has many good citizen friends who, for their own profit, follow the political machine and whoop it up for the trickster, electing him triumphantly.

Wherever the young man turns, expediency elbows principle into the gutter, with the help of those same self-styled good citizens. "Business is business"—and thereby we justify a market trick that sends a competitor to financial ruin and suicide. Soon the young man asks himself: "Why should I bend over backward to be honest?"

Love, he discovers, is a jest for television comedians; infidelity a gag for radio comics. He takes his best girl to the theater, and the leading lady of the smart new play tells her husband, whom she has long deceived with his best friend: "I am a better woman for the experience." The husband quite agrees, the audience claps its hands, and the curtain begins to fall on another ideal.

Other questions follow naturally. If loyalty in marriage

is old hat now, why then should one be loyal to friendship either, or to anything or anyone else, if it is more profitable not to be?

Seeing this increase in the tribe of cynics, one is tempted to agree with that old priest who wished "we could all be born old and grow younger and cleaner and ever simpler and more innocent, until at last, with the white souls of little children, we lay us down to eternal sleep."

The fault—the sin of all this—lies in us who have experienced such disillusion for ourselves. We must give bread to those who ask us and who now receive only a stone. No age has ever lacked its saints; in our bitterly disillusioned time they are still on earth, unselfishly at work; saints often without creed, yet consecrated, toiling in laboratories and jungles, pitting their lives against cancer and leprosy and all deadly plagues. It is for us, the elders, to hold up such men of the new kind of holiness as inspirers to dreamers everywhere. Instead of spilling the cold water of amused contempt on beautiful aspirations, let us feed the ardor of young fires. It is an act of damnation to rob the world of their warmth and light.

We must teach our youth more than letters and figures and diagrams. They must also be schooled in the kindly business of the heart, the affairs of soul and conscience, and the great basic fact that neither materialism nor mind is all there is to life.

When the millionaire Nicodemus sought out the Master in the dark and inquired the meaning of life, he was told that he must be born again. How can a man be born again? Most certainly here is one way: we can renew ourselves by strengthening and encouraging all the young dreamers, abetting them in the making of a better world. By helping them and refusing to harden and disenchant them, we shall find our own lost youth, our vanished faith, and shall know again the glory that was our birthright when we came from God, who is our home.

11

MARY OF DRUID HILL

*F*IRST I want to tell you how one woman I knew was able to hold onto her ideal, and then tell you what happened when another tried to elude God, once she had turned toward him.

The first of these two women was a friend of mine, and I have always called her Mary of Druid Hill.

My first clear memory of Mary Greenwillow is of a summer's day when she drove up in front of our house on Mosher Street in Baltimore. I can still see her descending from the canvas-topped wagon with the red-and-yellow wheels. On the curbstone she dropped a lump of lead tied to the reins of Sloppy, her mare. Then she crossed the mossy brick pavement and mounted our white marble steps.

"Son," she said to me, "what are you crying about?"

"Major is dead," I told her.

"Major who?"

"Major's my dog," I wailed.

"Where's your mom?" she demanded. When I brought mother to the door, Mary counted twelve eggs into our mixing bowl and laid a tissued pound of butter in with them. She was wearing a dark blue linen dress that morning, and the skirt reached to the instep. Her hat was of coarse black straw, and under the wide brim I could see her shining black hair, pale face, and immense eyes, black and lustrous as inkberries. She had the expression of a great lady in spite of large hands and feet.

"Look"—she spoke in a reasoning tone—"the kid's lost his dog. It's a whale of a big loss. Can I take him for a ride on the wagon? I'll get him a good lunch down at the market and have him home before suppertime. It'll sort of take his mind off things."

She allowed me to lift up the lead hitching weight and to keep my hands on the reins with hers as we went clip-clopping down Lafayette Avenue. At Argyle, she asked:

"What made Major die?"

Then I told Mary what I had not dared to tell my mother:

"I killed him!"

"You did?" said the butter and egg lady with tranquillity. "How?"

"Somebody threw a sample bottle of patent medicine in our vestibule."

"Yes?"

"I played Major was sick and I was the doctor. So I gave him the medicine."

"How much did you give him?"

"All of it," I sobbed.

At Division Street Mary Greenwillow pulled on the left rein and Sloppy turned the wagon around in a great half-moon. We were returning, but we stopped at our alley.

"Son," said Mary Greenwillow, "go bring me the dog."

Major was lying stiff in the sun behind our back-yard gate. I picked him up by his four paws and lugged him down to the wagon. Mary Greenwillow held his soft underparts against her ear.

"I don't believe he's dead," she declared. "I think that medicine just put him to sleep."

She rubbed his jowls with her palms. She coaxed and cajoled him. She told me to say the Lord's Prayer. And before I got started on it, Major opened one eye and yawned.

Thus began my intimacy with Mary Greenwillow, which lasted, I am glad to remember, until the end of her life. On many a summer's day I rode the whole route with her through Baltimore's leafy streets. I saw at firsthand how she lingered at house after house to yarn with the customers, and I defended her to my mother against the charge of dawdling. I knew, even then, that she was helping people out; she had a face that invited confidences and a heart that never betrayed them.

It was not until years later that I traced to the source her eager strength and wisdom. That was when she told me how she was born too soon. She had not known about it herself until her tenth birthday, when a certain Miss Timothy, superintendent of the orphan children's home, called the little girl into the office and gave her a letter from her mother:

Dear Mary:

I know you are going to be a girl and I want you to be called Mary. I am never going to see you; the pain around my heart tells me so. Dr. Mason has our money, and he has promised, if things do go wrong, that you will be taken care of by kind people. We are in a ship, you and I, anchored off a place called Fort McHenry. I want you to know that your father's name was Barry Ford and my name is Frances. We lived in Ballymote, not far from Sligo. Your father was a carpenter, and I was a schoolteacher before I was married. I always wanted to come to America, but your father was afraid. Never be afraid of anything, Mary. When he died, three months ago, I made up my mind to do it by myself. I wouldn't wait, because I wanted you to be born an American. But you're coming two months ahead of time. There is so much I want to tell you. In the U.S.A. you can raise yourself up even if you're poor. And remember, life will be grand and wonderful if you tell it to be and believe in it. If God lets me, I'll be near you all the time.

Lovingly,
Mother

"You're taking a long time with the letter," complained Miss Timothy.

Mary clutched the paper. Soundlessly she was repeating her mother's words. From that moment on she knew the letter by heart; fifty years later she repeated it to me like a litany. Then began a wonderful game of solitaire—the secret pleasure of trying to imagine what her mother had looked like. Did the invisible face resemble Miss Timothy? Or was it like the blue-and-gold statue of the Mother of God? Or the little Dutch girl on the can of cocoa in the kitchen?

By the time she was fifteen Mary decided that her mother had looked like herself. She was a tall girl, with strong legs and busy stride; she had creamy skin, and her hair was pulled back straight and wound in a coil at the nape of the neck.

"An Irish biddy with a touch of brimstone," Mr. Carter said. Mr. Carter was the head of the first family for which Mary went to work; he lurked in the hallways and slapped her on the buttocks. But it was not brimstone; what was in the hired girl was a simple and irresistible satisfaction with the gift of life itself.

"Earth," she wanted to shout, "you are wonderful. Days and nights, you are going to be grand, and I believe in you."

And while she passed briskly upstairs and down in all her scrubbing and dusting and sweeping, she cherished within a sharp excited sympathy with the boat whistles from the harbor and the rumblings and blowings of trains, the smell of heady perfumes from the open doors of shops, and the sight of grand ladies behind prancing horses and gleaming harness. To all families for whom she toiled she felt alien, until she went to work for the Leverings.

The Leverings lived in a house that fronted on Druid Hill Park. The very words had a musical sound to Mary and she asked what the name meant. Mr. Levering looked it up, the first use he had ever made of his twenty-volume encyclopedia, and that night at dinner table he took succulent delight in lecturing the household on menhirs and dolmens and the priest of ancient Gaul performing heathen rites in the moonlight.

Long years afterward Mary told me how often, at night, when the housework was done, she walked alone through the tall groves of Druid Hill and breathed deep of the dark, sweet dampness, and tried to imagine what her future life would be like. Someday, she made up her mind, she would have a husband, and a family, and a home that looked upon the park. From such walks she would come back with renewed enthusiasm for the way the Leverings lived, and a desire to learn from them. It was a confusing world; they jabbered about concerts and whist and Bryan and McKinley and Thomas Hardy and Eddie Foy. They

went to church on Sunday, but they were not solemn for
the rest of the holiday; they played the gramophone and
went for buggy rides, and the funny papers were communal
property. A Sabbath box of candy was always open to all
on the sideboard. Mary's memories were compounded of
Hail, Mary, and Foxy Grandpa, and down the years she
could smell incense and peanut brittle.

She was not quite eighteen when James Hamilton
Greenwillow walked into the Levering kitchen. He was
wearing tall black boots, brown corduroy trousers, a hunting shirt of blue-and-white plaid, open at the neck, and a
coonskin cap. One hand held a basketful of eggs; the other
a scoop of butter.

"Mind your dirty feet on my nice kitchen floor!" cried
Mary, turning unreasonably red. She liked this man at
once, taking in his pug nose and long ears and red face and
boylike blue eyes. And she smiled when he insisted on
shaking hands and informed her that he was a black sheep.

"I always like to tell people first," he explained. "If they
want to go on knowing me after that, it's their own dag-
gone fault."

Jim was the last twig on a dead family tree; by royal grant
his people had once owned a valley in Carroll County.

"I was never meant to work, but I do, just the same."
He grinned, then slapped his legs with both palms,
squinched up his nose, showed white teeth and a doggy
red tongue while his body quaked with laughter.

"How much does Mr. Sickelfram pay you for running
the butter-and-egg route?" she asked him. That was on her
afternoon off, some weeks later, and she was riding beside
him on the front seat of the wagon.

"Oh, he gives me my board and keep and a couple of

dollars whenever I need it," Jim answered, humble and offhand.

"You ought to be running your own route, working for yourself," she told him boldly.

But Jim looked off at the treetops overhanging the sidewalk and shook his head.

"I wouldn't know how to do anything like that."

"In the U.S.A. you can raise yourself up," she insisted.

"Have I got a farm? Have I got chickens and cows? Have I got a horse and wagon? Have I got customers?"

He pleaded at the bar of common sense, demanding a verdict in favor of his own ineffectuality. But late that night Mary wrapped her cloak around her and walked through the lonely groves of Druid Hill Park. She was consulting her spirit, playing her old game of trying to see the face of the unknown future. She went to bed full of energy and confidence, and the next morning asked Mrs. Levering if she might take the morning off.

Down at the bank Mr. Levering was astounded to learn that his hired girl was in the anteroom and would like to see him.

"I couldn't help hearing you talk one night at supper table how you lent some money to the railroad," Mary began. "I wondered if I could borrow some too. I want to buy a horse and wagon."

"That was how," Mary told me, "Mr. Levering became my business adviser." Under his coaching Jim came to terms with Mr. Sickelfram, who agreed to sell him butter and eggs at fair wholesale prices. To get a new route Jim walked miles of city blocks, ringing doorbells and soliciting customers. They took their time and found a bargain in horse and wagon.

Within two years their debts were paid off. Jim was earning a clear profit of twenty dollars a week from his business. That was when Mary Ford became Mrs. Greenwillow at the altar of St. Anne's on Greenmount Avenue.

Their first home was a flat, far from Druid Hill Park, of course, but Mary was happy in those rooms, because Jim was her perfect and completely satisfying companion. They knew a mutual joy, and their days and nights were vigorous and full of laughter. Jim had no taste for other women, nor for gambling—and he liked to work hard. His temptation was the saloon. In the beginning Mary drank with him, but not after she had conceived. Twice, while she was carrying her first child, she was called by a bartender; Jim was snoring drunk, with the wagon hitched outside. Both times she arranged with the saloonkeeper's wife to put Jim to bed, while she climbed on the driver's seat and completed the deliveries of butter and eggs. And no repining, no self-pity. She forgave her husband with almost indecent haste so that they could get back to their lives.

"Child," she would cry to her unborn baby, "you are wonderful. Your future is going to be grand, and I believe in you."

There were two children, James and Frances. When Jim talked about his son taking over the route someday, Mary hid her smile behind big hands. Already she knew that her son would go to college; he was quick and sure in school. And he was a good boy, she told herself. As the time approached for his First Communion, Mary bought him a new suit, a lovely white dress for Frances, and sewed for herself a made-over but handsome frock. Jim's Sunday suit was carefully pressed for the proud occasion, but Jim did not come home until the dawn of that Sabbath, and then he threw himself on the bed without taking off his clothes.

Mary stood and looked at him and said:

"Jim, you're going to church with the rest of us."

When a deep snoring snarl answered her, she attacked him. She clawed at the mighty bulk of his body until she had turned him over. She poured a pitcher of icewater down his neck, rubbed him with a crash towel, shook him unmercifully, forced scalding coffee down his throat, and dragged him, grunting and swearing, to the tub. She flooded him first with hot water, then with cold, and heaved in a fifty-pound cake of ice from the kitchen refrigerator. The bewildered descendant of aristocrats bleated and wept, but he sobered. With trembling hands he shaved. Wearing his Sunday suit, he marched with his wife and children to St. Anne's and sat in a front pew, under a stained-glass window with a scarlet light from St. Joseph's cloak garnishing his thinning hair.

On the way home he was sullen.

"You leave me alone after this," he warned. "I told you I was a black sheep. I would have got myself there if you had only let me alone."

A part of Mary told her he spoke the truth. She felt alarmed for having been false to something universal and fine, a spiritual precocity that hitherto had stayed her tongue from scolding; for she knew that she must not bind this man with a sense of guilt, but let him loose and free, and believe in him. They did not clash again until the day that Jim remarked:

"Won't be long now before little Jim can take over the wagon."

"Jim's going to Johns Hopkins and be a doctor," Mary announced.

Whereupon the father squinched up his nose and showed white teeth and lolling tongue, convulsed in the mocking and hopeless laughter of the unfit. Unabashed, Mary calmly unfolded her plan:

"We can sell the butter-and-egg route now. It's worth a lot, and I've already found a man who wants to buy it."

"Who wants to sell it?"

"We do, honey. Listen! We'll get enough money to put Jim through Johns Hopkins and Frances through Bryant and Stratton Business College and still have enough left for ourselves to open a little store. We can sell bread and milk and ice cream and cakes and candy; I know a nice location near a public school. You can mind the store and I can do nursing in confinement cases; you know I'm good at that."

The only question Jim asked was the name of the man who wanted to buy the route. A few nights later he came home with the announcement that the deal was made, the money passed, the route sold. But that was not all. He had spent the cash already on something that he had wanted all his life, a saloon of his own.

It was a sticky day in the inferno of Baltimore heat when Jim broke the news like a bottle over her head. Dark eyes shut, Mary held on stiffly to the arm of the parlor sofa. Where was this saloon? Darbyholt Street? Why, that wasn't a street at all. It was just a narrow lane, two blocks long, that ran from Perkins Square to Pennsylvania Avenue. A colored slum.

"I like it there," Jim blazed. "The people don't put on airs."

For days she was silent as a sleepwalker. Her concern was about sending the children to college, and now she could see no way to pay. Most of the time Jim was away; at night he came home with red and blue paint on his hands and gilt on his eyebrows; he was redecorating for a grand reopening of his barroom on Saturday night.

Monday morning a policeman came to the front door. She had better go down to the saloon; Jim had been his own best customer.

"That," Mary told me, "was when I committed my greatest sin."

Old Negro men and women in Darbyholt Street still remember that Monday morning. Jim was lying on top of the bar under a mirror with a gilded frame. Mary rolled up her sleeves and with desolate resolution went to work. Fifty bottles of rotgut liquor she poured out in the street; keg after keg of beer she rolled through the swinging doors, pulled out the bung stops and emptied foaming streams into the gutter. From the houses the people came swarming; they toted tin cans and milk bottles to catch some of the spill.

Eventually Jim came home. He packed a suitcase, put on his hat and strode out, and Mary never saw him again.

She felt his going like the removal of an eye. How could she tell the earth to be grand and the days and nights to be wonderful? All that seemed left to her was resolution. The boy must not take a job as he cried to do; he must go to medical school. Frances must have her business course. Back Mary went to Mr. Levering, to Mr. Sickelfram, to the livery stable. She borrowed money for school and money for her business, and for weeks she tramped the streets, gathering customers for a new route of her own.

In that dark time, on endless drives from house to house, Mary learned how much she had loved Jim. She had asserted her will over him, and that, she knew, was wrong.

"I finally realized," she told me, "that I could have bought Sloppy, started my route—I could have done everything that I did anyway—and still I needn't have bothered Jim. It nearly drove me crazy to know that."

She wondered if other human beings were as blind as she had been. It was misery's need for company that made her pry. She began slyly asking questions of her customers about their private lives. Why do you look so down today, Mrs. Steinkampf? Where did you get that black eye, Mrs. Kelly? Son, what are you crying for? Major is dead!

We did not dislike her for her questions. We warmed to her interest and responded to her counsels. Her consolations lay in prompt and sensible action; we must agree with our adversary quickly while we were in the way with him, forgiving not seven times but seventy times seven, as we ourselves hoped to be forgiven, lest we destroy the bridge over which we had to cross. In all such wisdom Mary was talking to herself—too late. Your unmarried daughter is in the family way, Mrs. Reid? Go quickly and put your arms around her; that is the first thing to do.

But while Mary gave good counsel, it was always strong; never pietistic nor mealymouthed. For example, there was young Cliff Chester, who had come up to the city from one of the river towns along the eastern shore of Maryland. Cliff was a builder of small sailing boats; that was his trade, and his heart was in it. But one summer a Baltimore girl, spending her vacation near Queenstown, stood and watched Cliff making a ship and asked him questions, so that he fell in love with her. In the city, she told him, carpenters were paid five times what he earned on the eastern shore. So they were married and came to live on Myrtle Avenue, only a few "squares," as we say, from my home. The back-fence talk was that Cliff and Gertrude were happy, all but for one thing. The wife wanted to go dancing and to euchre parties after supper, but Cliff was restless unless he could plunge into the cellar of their two-story house and work for hours on a boat that he had started a month after they moved in.

"I saw the thing," Mary Greenwillow told me. "He laid the keel, and the wood was white and shaped so perfectly you knew it was right for the water."

One night Mary and I drove up in front of Cliff's house and found the carpenter sitting on the front marble steps in a trance of dismay. While making change for a dozen eggs, she extracted the story:

"We've busted up. She says she's tired of living with a fool, and I don't much blame her. Tonight I finished my boat down in the cellar. Then I found out what she knew all the time: the boat was so big there was no way to get it out. Gertie stood at the top of the cellar steps and laughed. Now she's upstairs, packing."

"Do you really love her?" Mary asked. "No kidding yourself?"

"Yep," answered Cliff. "No kidding, I really do."

"Only trouble with her is she don't know what it is to have a boat in your heart. Let's tear the house apart and get it out."

And Mary presently drove away, clucking her tongue at Sloppy, and behind us I heard the noise of an ax falling against bricks. Cliff Chester smashed a great rent in the front of his home and drew out his unpainted ship like a living thing from a womb. Gertrude, watching from the upper window, was filled with fear and respect for the man. The two of them hired a truck and drove the little ship down to Back River, where they launched it late that night.

"It was easy for Cliff to repair that wall," Mary said to me. "It was hard for him to break it down, though. I'm glad they're happy now."

She became an institution on her route. Her prosperity was only an incident. Earth was grand and days and nights were wonderful, because she had shown us how to make them that, dishing out practical common sense to the tormented and the distracted as a premium that came free of all charge with the eggs and butter. Mary Greenwillow at the reins drove from door to door about her Father's business.

"Mom," said Jim one day, "we've saved up enough now. I don't like you driving, rain, heat, cold, all the whole year around. I am ready to open my office and I can take care of you."

"I like it," said Mary. "It's wonderful."

"Mom," said Frances, "my boss has asked me to marry him. I'm going to be Mrs. Teitelbaum. And you're not going to work any more."

And she tried to explain to her mother that Mr. Teitelbaum was soon going to run for Congress and it mightn't look well, the wagon route and all.

"It will get him votes," promised Mary.

After a while, she told me with a grin, they stopped protesting. Jim was getting to have a good practice. Mr. Teitelbaum was elected and took Frances to live in Washington. One magic night Mary, in a new black dress, was taken to the congressional reception at the White House; she shook hands with the President and danced in the East Room with a naval officer. But the next day she was driving her route.

Jim bought a house opposite Druid Hill Park soon after his marriage, and Mary was coaxed to live there. The reality of her old dream coming true was not a thrill but a pleasant experience; she still loved to walk alone under the tall trees and question the unseen.

I remember her in one of those latter days, driving through a spring rain; her hair was gray and her face was wrinkling, but her immense eyes were still lustrous, and she had the air of a great lady, in spite of big hands and feet. There were grown grandchildren by then: the sons and daughters of the junior Greenwillows, and of the Teitelbaums, preparing their own marriages.

"I suppose," she told Jim one day, when she was recovering from a nasty siege of the flu, "I have enough of my own family to talk to now; the time has come for me to sell out my business."

But she lived only a year afterward. At the last there was a large family circled around the bedside; among them a granddaughter who had married a Communist who was doing a term in jail, another engaged to the owner of a department store, and a third the wife of a tent evangelist.

"She was unconscious," Dr. Greenwillow told me, "but her lips began to move. They all thought Mother was praying, but I knew better."

So did I. I knew that she was saying:

"Death, you are wonderful! God and Heaven, you are going to be grand, and I believe in you."

12

A BARGAIN IN BRIMSTONE

*T*HEN there was that other woman, one I never saw, but whose history, so full of evil and wonder, was told to me over coffee cups one night at a dinner in Washington.

It began, long ago, in a poor Chicago parish. The young assistant to the pastor had been warned that his new assignment, "back of the yards" in the abattoir quarter, would be a nightmare job. In that region of bull pens, slaughterhouses, and slums there was more delinquency than in all the rest of the town, poverty and ignorance in the flats begetting crime in the streets.

One muggy afternoon in deep July he sat in the airless chamber of the confessional. Out of doors the mercury neared 100 degrees; in the covered recess where he listened in darkness it was hotter still. His neck and wrists were moist; his body, swathed in a cassock down to his shoes, winced with prickly heat—and still, on both sides of the box, men and women stood in lines and waited.

Finally, during a brief lull, the young priest stepped out of the confession cabinet to get a breath of air. As he blinked at the light of the open door, a whiff of perfume startled him. Who was making the church smell like a beauty parlor? He turned, and the odor rushed toward him, a polluting mixture of heliotrope and vanilla. The sweetish smell was a little sickening; then he heard the husky whisper of a girl:

"Take it easy, big boy. I didn't come in here on religious business, so you can relax!"

Dimly he could discern her outline standing in the shadows under a tiny window; her face was invisible.

"What are you here for?" he demanded.

"To kill time," she replied with a bumptious giggle.

"Well, this is a good way to kill time—if you really like it dead." And then he added grimly: "But why?"

"Oh, I just promised my old lady I would come to church and pray, that's all. She's waiting outside. Could I get in the confessional for a while? I only want to stay here about five minutes, to let her think I'm going through with it. But no confession, you understand!"

The priest mopped his dripping forehead, cleared his throat cautiously, and began:

"Listen, child——"

"Call me Aggie. That's my name. Aggie Retzinek."

"I am not asking your name," he said, "but I will tell you it's Russian—Agafia. It's a Greek word—and do you know what it means? It means good."

Her snorting chuckle was throttled down by the fear of being overheard.

"That's a joke on you, big boy. Let me tell you something. *I'm* the worst girl in this town."

"Oh no you're not."

"Oh yes I am."

"Oh no you're *not!* I *know* the worst girl in this town."

"And who is she?"

"She's the girl who thinks she is the *best* girl in town." There was a remote banter in his tone. "You know, I might make your confession for you."

"Okay, wise guy! Let's hear you do it—and a buck says you'll flop!"

In one glance the man of God took her in—a short-necked, long-eyed girl whose frizzled hair was tied in pink bows. The eldritch face was aged in experience, yet hopelessly young and futile; catlike eyes looked at him in steadfast contempt. She was weaving and twining her fingers together with a faint jingle of bracelets, and there flashed through his mind the lines of Eleanor Wylie:

> I am, being a woman, hard beset;
> I live, by squeezing from a stone
> The little nourishment I get.

"I see," he muttered sadly.

"Sure! Now you've looked me over, you know!"

Her voice, husky as it was, lacked the usual brothel coarseness; it was more like the voice of a child with a cold.

"Wouldn't you like to know why I still say I am the worst girl?" she asked.

"You could never convince me of such a thing."

"Can't I though! Listen, big boy—I just got out of the state reformatory for girls. *Reformatory!*"

She spewed out the word, disgorging with it a torrent of profanity. The young priest clutched damp hands together, fiercely reminding himself that he could never befriend this girl if he lost his temper.

"I fell for your holy stuff at first," she went on. "All I cared about was getting out of there. So I went to chapel and I prayed to God. But He must have been too busy for the likes of me."

"Perhaps He said no."

"Have it any way you want. I didn't go free, that's all."

"Go on."

"Are you sure you want to know?"

"Of course."

"All right. You asked for it. I made a prayer to the devil!"

Even in the gloom of the church she could see the blanched face and the wondering eyes of the perspiring priest. Here was an unfamiliar transgression indeed: *diablerie*, faith turned wickedly upside down!

"But the devil," he prodded quietly; "doesn't he always ask a price?"

"Why shouldn't he? Don't you? I promised him, if he would only get me out of that place, I would make nine sacrilegious communions. I did too. I took communion and I cursed God! Plenty! And you know what? On the eighth time I got paroled. So now, big boy—what do you say to that?"

In three universities the priest had worked for scholarly degrees. He was considered a well-educated—even a sophisticated—man. Yet at this atrocious disclosure he felt as if in the bodiless presence of Evil itself. Tremulous, quavering, he heard himself answering:

"I say he got a good bargain, that's what I say! This devil you prayed to, he gives you what you call freedom and in exchange he gets an immortal soul. That is a wonderful thing—the immortal soul of a child of God. But——"

"Don't get yourself so worked up, big boy."

"You're cheating the devil—and I thank God for it. There's still time!"

"Look here, I never broke a bargain with anybody! Never!"

"Your soul is not lost—not yet."

"How dare you say such a thing to me?" she cried in a sudden, tearful rage.

"What are you in this church for? To please your mother! That means your mother is still dear to you. And don't you see that no one who loves can be hopelessly lost? Remain here with me—and all this can be blotted out like a bad dream."

A faint moan came from her. He could see her writhe, as if her whole body were contorted in the grip of some violent emotion; her breath came in gasps and the bracelets jangled.

"That's enough!" she panted. "I'm getting out. You can't do nothing to me!"

"Stay here and pray!" pleaded the priest.

She turned her back on him.

"You'll come back!" he declared, "tonight!"

He could hear the click-clock of high heels pattering down the aisle, out to the flagstones of the vestibule, and down the marble steps into the sunlit inferno of the street.

Back in the confessional he sat on the stool, pale but full of faith. This trollop child could not be lost! The sticky reek of her scent plagued his nostrils, and he could still hear her strumpet laughter and angry weeping. It seemed to him then as if this tiny box of space were a microcosm of the vast, bewildering macrocosm; as if this confused and sweltering little area contained all there was of Heaven, earth, the bottomless pit, everywhere, and the struggle of good and evil dumped in his lap. No matter how, he must fight harder than ever against the diabolic power of self-interest and the processes of corruption.

The thing had happened. It was not a fantasy. That compact had all the impossible and awful logic of a dream; Aggie Retzinek truly believed she had signed up in sulphur and brimstone—and who was he to underestimate the force of such a belief? He prayed for guidance.

Yet from the first the answer had been clear. The only way to fight was with the weapons of the soul, which are love and prayer. He turned again to listen to confidences of anxiety and loneliness and distress. All the penitents were given their prayers, and then, to one after another, he said:

"I ask you now to help the pastor of this church to pray for a special need. Will you stay for one hour in the church and pray?"

None refused. One man postponed a journey; others broke off appointments. Some volunteered to stay all afternoon. Soon the pews were spotted with parishioners praying for someone and something of which they knew nothing.

When afternoon and evening confessions were over at last, the priest came out of the stifling box.

"Every one like her was a virgin once," he whispered to himself as he walked up the aisle toward the altar. The last shafts of the twilight arch pierced the open door behind him, and the tall colored windows of rainbow saints and tinted miracles splashed his path with pale light. He began to feel the addition of some new strangeness to the hour. Kneeling, he laid hot palms on the firm coolness of the marble balustrade. From the street came the distant calls of late hucksters, crying strawberries and water-melons, as he began the first Our Father.

Hour after hour dragged by. Night dusk came late, with the glimmer of flickering candle flames and the ringing of the tower bells. The street noises dimmed and soon the church was abandoned of all except the enrapt friend of Agatha Retzinek. Once there clanged out a siren and there was the rumble of hook and ladders rolling to a fire, but the kneeling figure did not seem to hear.

At last the church was emptied for the night, except for the one praying figure. He was still keeping solitary vigil when a sexton shuffled in to put out the lights and close the doors.

"Never mind!" called the priest. "I'll lock up," and bowed his head again in his long bivouac of prayer.

It was well after midnight when he heard the click-clock of heels coming down the marble aisle. Hope surged in his soul—and then a last, pallid whiff of perfume made him gasp with joyous certainty. He did not move or look around as she knelt beside him, but he heard her begin to weep.

"If I had not waited for her," the priest told me, "she would have found the doors locked and would have turned away, perhaps never to come back. Agatha is a wonderful girl today."

I have told this story to men of many faiths, and the feelings of all were summed up in what Harry Emerson Fosdick said:

"I salute this priest! He is a real servant of Christ, this Monsignor Fulton J. Sheen!"

13

THE MISTAKE

*I*N THE attempt to serve the Heavenly Father, one soon learns the wisdom of that ancient, scriptural phrase which tells us that God moves in a mysterious way His wonders to perform. Like my friend Brown, of Newport, New Hampshire. I give you his story as he told it to me:

That night I would have sworn that I was the only waking soul in town. By ten o'clock in those old days most of the inhabitants of West Princeton, Washington County, in the state of Maine, blew out their lamps, but at midnight I was far from asleep, spellbound by a book. It was the work of a modern atheistic philosopher who saw life as a madhouse, without meaning or hope. Deep in the materialistic argument, I jumped when suddenly someone came rapping on the porch screen.

The raven at Poe's chamber door could not have come tapping more insistently. Oil lamp in hand, I found, on the front steps, a woman from the lower crossroads, a stolid farm wife with black hair and eyes and sunburned face.

"What's wrong, Jane?" I asked. We had the same last name of Brown, she and I, and we were friends. Only two weeks before, I had heard, her husband had been brought home after an operation.

"It's my man. He thinks he's going to die, Bill."

"Did he have a relapse?"

"You know Tom—too much hurry to get back to plowing, so he ruptured the incision. An ambulance is on the way over now to take him back to the hospital; it'll get here in about an hour. Tom can't wait to talk to you before they take him."

Still under the spell of my midnight book, enchanted with the audacity and logic of atheism, I was the last person in our township to counsel a dying man, but I knew perfectly well why Tom Brown had sent his wife to fetch me.

In his mind I was the nearest thing to a preacher in our township. Like all the other four hundred residents, he expected that I would be going off to divinity school in September, and that someday I would come back to open the town's first church. For that purpose my older sister had skimped and saved, and at her deathbed I had told her I would be a parson. But I knew now that I could never keep that promise. College had opened my eyes; my outlook had grown increasingly skeptical, until finally I realized I had lost my last shred of faith. In September I would be leaving to travel the world, working my way, and I meant to have a high old time doing it. What could I, who no longer believed in the existence of the soul, of immortality, or God, have to say to Tom Brown as he lay facing death?

"Maybe Tom is right about going to die," Mrs. Brown pleaded. "You won't mind coming so late, will you?"

THE MISTAKE 153

It would have been cruel to refuse, or to lecture on my
views, there on the moonlit porch. Because it seemed the
natural thing, I slipped into my pocket the small Testament my sister had given me; on the flyleaf she had written my name in her firm, strong hand.

"I'll just read to him," I told myself. "That won't compromise my convictions."

In silence I set off with Mrs. Brown down the narrow
footway. On the lawn of the crossroads house Tom
Brown's young son was waiting. He was a tall, strong
youth, with his mother's black eyes and hair. He told me
his father wanted to talk in private. Although the night
was moist and warm, the sick man was cowering under a
heap of blankets, face damp and pale.

"Reverend!" he murmured.

"Tom," I smiled, taking his shivering hand, "you know
I'm no reverend."

"Not official, naturally," he said, nodding solemnly.
"But in your heart you're already the real thing, and if
you don't help me out, I'm a man that's done for!"

I leaned over so that I could hear all that he whispered.

"I'm scared to hell and back. I never killed nobody, or
stole any money, but I've been mighty mean to my wife
and my boy, and I've never paid no attention to God, what-
sumever. Never prayed, never gave anything to charity.
Always too busy making a living; never could seem to find
the time. Now I'm in for it. I know I can't live through
another operation, and before it's too late I want to make
it clear I'm sorry. Reverend—I'm awful scared to die . . ."

I pitied the poor man, but had no compassion for him,
and there is a world of difference. I did not suffer *with*

him; to me his terror seemed degrading, and turned me a little sick. A dog dies like a dog, I thought; why can't a man die like a man?

But in his groveling panic he did need help, and so, taking the Testament from my pocket, I began to read:

" 'He hath sent me to heal the brokenhearted . . . to set at liberty them that are bruised. . . . Death is swallowed up in victory. . . . In my Father's house are many mansions . . . I go to prepare a place for you. . . . And God shall wipe away all tears . . . there shall be no more death, neither sorrow, nor crying, neither shall there be any more pain . . .' "

On and on I read, until there came to Tom Brown's face a look of profound relief.

"Reverend, could you do one thing more for me?" he asked huskily. "Let me have the loan of this book for a while? I want to carry it with me."

"Sure!" I told him. "I have no use for it any more."

Within an hour Tom Brown was on his way back to the hospital at St. Stephen in New Brunswick, which lay just across the St. Croix River and the international boundary, thirty miles away.

I returned to my home, and, reading no more that night, soon entered a dreamless sleep. Lost to the world, I lay there, all unaware of a curious and tragic mix-up thirty miles away, by which Tom Brown's death and the rest of my life were soon to be linked in fantastic partnership. Long after sunup I was roused by another knocking: young Michael Brown, pale and uncombed.

"Dad died under the ether," the youth blurted out. He sat on the sofa and fiddled with his cap, as with all the earnestness of seventeen years he said:

"He carried your Bible right into the operating room. Would you let us bury it with him? Thanks, Bill! They will bring Dad home tonight, and Mom thought——"

"Just a minute, Mike," I said. "I'll do anything I can to help you and your mother—but I can't conduct services or anything like that."

He lifted his hand reassuringly.

"You don't have to hold back because you're not a minister yet," he said. "Everybody understands."

"Mike, listen." I laid my hand on his shoulder; there was only three years' difference in our ages. "I'm not going to be a minister. I don't believe in religion any more."

"Even when things go wrong, you don't need anybody?"

"Man has to be strong enough to stand alone in the world." I was uncomfortably aware of sounding oracular and dogmatic, for all my scorn of such things.

"And you think it's all over for Dad?—that we're never going to see him again?"

"Your father's out of his misery and that's something to be glad of," I said, rising from the sofa.

But Mike did not stand up with me. He sat, huddled and hurt.

"What are we going to do?" he asked, more of himself than of me. "Other people are not bold like you are. When things go wrong we want somebody to buck us up, not kick us in the teeth."

"This community has its leaders," I said. "What's wrong with old Doc Taylor? He's a great comfort to everybody. And the schoolteacher——"

"Sure, Reverend," Mike said doggedly. "They're kind and smart all right. But they're busy too. We need somebody who hasn't anything else to do but keep us bucked up and on the right track. Your sister told us we could count on *you*—and you said so too. How can you back down now?"

He walked up to me and his eyes were smoldering.

"You're going to hold some kind of service over my dad —I don't care how you think. I'm not going back to Mom——"

He would have tried to thrash me, I felt sure—and right then I would not have cared. Michael Brown had set off in me a volcano, a conflict of emotion and thought, of heart and conscience.

"Tell your mother it's all right," I said. "Better not let her know how I feel."

And with tormented mind I watched the tall, round-shouldered figure stalking homeward. . . .

There was, at the head of our street, a wooden chapel which I had helped to build during the summer two years before, and I had painted it. Sometimes a city minister, on vacation somewhere near, would conduct worship there. On this June afternoon I stood on the pulpit steps, the open coffin in the aisle, my Testament in folded hands, as I faced the family and neighbors.

What was I going to say to them? My heart was touched by their grief, but my obstinate brain regarded this ceremony as folly. I was determined to be kind and helpful, but no words of mine should ever be a sop to fear, a shoddy appeal to baseless hope; I wanted to comfort them, yet not deceive them. I almost prayed to God to help me not to let them think I believed in Him.

"Dearly beloved," I began, "we are gathered this afternoon to pay our last respects to one who lies here in death;

a man known to all of us for most of our lives, our lost neighbor——"

I paused, aware within myself of a sense of great conflict and heartache all my own. In that moment of hesitation I let my glance fall to the gleaming brass name plate of the coffin. Then my brain reeled.

The name on the plate was William F. Brown. And that was *my* name!

A dizziness overwhelmed me; the room, the mourners, the coffin itself seemed to sway and grow dim. For one moment of panic I had the horrible conviction that it was my body lying there, while I, a disembodied soul, was looking on, a ghost at my own funeral. And I was mortally afraid— just as afraid as poor Tom Brown had been when he begged me to help him. In that awful instant my pride crumbled and all my intellectual arrogance; I knew I could not stand alone. Humility seemed to flood my being with a great fear, and my doubts dissolved with my conceit; in that awful instant I could feel with Tom and with every other frightened soul in the world; for I, too, needed help. I needed reassurance; I wanted God.

For a moment I just stood there, shaken and tongue-tied. Not until later was I to learn how the undertaker had sought the name and thought he had found it on the fly-leaf of my Testament. Now I did not try to solve the mystery; the solemnity of death consumed me, and the need for courage—the simple, mortal cry for comfort.

My voice came back to me and I began falteringly:

"We have been told that man was made with a soul and partakes of immortality. No man has ever lived who could prove that this was not true. We have the choice of faith, of believing that it is so. For we have been told that 'he that believeth, though he be dead, yet shall he live again.' "

Later I stood by the open grave and watched the sunset light make a fiery badge of my name plate as it was lowered into the earth.

"Bill," the widow said on the way home, "your words have helped me. You *are* sure, aren't you?"

"Jane, I never felt so sure before."

In September I left for theological school. All the rest of my life I have served as a small-town minister. And I thank God that I have never been anything else. Today I am pastor of the First Baptist Church of Newport, New Hampshire. And there is no part of my work that I practice with more conviction than the consolation of the bereaved; for even today, as on that long-ago afternoon at the grave, I feel like one who died and rose again.

Thus the tale, as Pastor Brown told it to me.

14

WHY LOVE MY ENEMY?

*H*E WHO truly knows God knows perfect love, and by that perfect experience fear and hatred are cast out of the heart. We are told to love our enemies, but we can do that only when we know God.

To hate an enemy is to conspire with him for our own defeat. That is because hatred is a destructive adviser which blinds the reason, corrupts the judgment, and visits upon the body various and painful ailments.

But to love an enemy is a kind of exquisite common sense. It is the height of selflessness, whose enlightened wisdom nourishes the well-being of body, mind, and spirit.

The counsels of the Sermon on the Mount do not ask too much of human nature, but often we fail to grasp their hard-bitten practicality. Christ was not seeking to make weaklings when He said: "I come bringing not peace, but a sword." All men, both in private life and in public affairs, are called upon to take sides in the never-ending clash between justice and oppression. But that is a call for strength, and Christ knew what modern psychiatry has only rediscovered—that most men are destroyed not by their enemies but by themselves.

Four hundred years before Christ was born, Hippocrates, first great savant of medicine, declared that hatred and fear are like poisons in the blood. As psychosomatic medicine now teaches, such poisons can produce ulcers and arthritis and even more terrifying ills. To be safe, we need the courage to love.

Greatest of the French kings, Henry IV, threw food over the walls of Paris every night during his long siege of the city. When at last he conquered them, the people pelted him with flowers of welcome, knowing he had never hated them and that they need not fear him.

Hatred, pretending to be a friend, is really our Judas, always ready to betray us into defeat. Loving the enemy is a matter of attitude and purpose; of how we think and feel about what we are doing; of fighting for an ideal that we love, and not merely crushing someone that we hate. Once free of bitterness, our strength is as the strength of ten, because then the heart is pure.

In defeat and helplessness there can still be dignity and serenity. Long ago my father tried to teach me this spiritual courtesy. I remember standing with him at the window when the widow who lived next door was walking past our house. In her hand she carried a nosegay of her backyard flowers.

"She has only a Civil War pension to live on, and yet last week her rent was raised," my father told me. "That's why she's carrying the flowers—to show the landlord there's no hard feelings. She always acts like that—and it's a great way to live!"

"Why?" I demanded. I wanted to throw rocks at the landlord.

"Because," my father said, "it's hard to hate a man you

give flowers to. She needs to be able to think calmly about how to find a little extra money every month. I'll bet the bouquet won't mean a damn thing to that old skinflint, but to her it can make all the difference in the world."

I was too young then to realize how hatred tears at the heart with frenzied claws; how self-pity can paralyze self-reliance. Boylike, it seemed only natural that if someone blacked my eye, I should bloody his nose. But as I grew older, and the pushing around in life became more so-phisticated, I found that retaliation and revenge wasted valuable time; it is better to co-operate with the inevitable and make the best of things as they are. Now I prefer aggressive fighting for those causes I believe in, without either the cold malice that corrodes body and mind, or the bitter passion that rends us. That *is* a great way to live, and its reward is inner peace. To remain master of the soul's household is to be like the sandalwood tree, which remains truly itself even in violence and death and im-parts its fragrance even to the blade of the ax that cuts it down.

One afternoon not long ago I sat before a wood fire and drank green tea with a Chinese lady whom I have known for many years. As I watched the warm light play across her face, I wondered at the tranquillity of her expression and the peace in her eyes. Most of all, I marveled that she spoke of the enemies of her country without bitterness. Yet she had lived through the thousand-and-seven bomb-ings of Chungking.

"Surely," I said, "you must feel a resentment against the Chinese Reds. I should think you would hate *us* for not having helped you more. As for the Japs——"

She smiled. "No, I can't even hate the Japs. I am not

being noble. I am talking only about the common sense of the soul."

And then she told me the tale of her desperate misadventure, which taught her the hardest and best lesson she had ever learned.

It happened in Chungking in the season of the full moon. There is no fairer scene of peace than a Chinese countryside under a round bright moon, but in war the lovely silver light shows the way to enemy planes, making day of the night, and there is bombing all around the clock.

My Chinese friend would be busy about her own affairs. Then the signal would sound. She would hurry down into the shelters, under the Yellow Mountain rock that stands like Gibraltar where two rivers flow together, beyond the temporary capital. The caves were dark, and there was only candlelight; in the chill and damp, with water incessantly dribbling down the rocky walls, the people huddled together in a democracy of common danger: cook and general, coolie and priest.

They could hear the muffled explosions and feel the rough stone floor tremble under their feet as the bombs fell on homes and churches and orphanages. When at last the "all-clear" whistle blew, they would climb the long dark corridor that led to the clear air and the sunlight. There would be a little time to put out the fires, carry in the wounded, lift the dead from the streets before the alarm would scream again, calling all back to the shelter.

And during the season of the bright moon, that experience was repeated twenty-four times a day.

My friend was never once afraid, nor did she hate, even then. From childhood she had been raised as a Christian, taught to forgive, and to do good even to those who did evil to her. And while, like the rest of us, she often fell short of such ideals, she knew that grudges and desires for revenge were poison to the soul. Nor had it ever occurred to her that she could ever be attracted to such poison.

But that was before she found herself in a beleaguered city, especially in the time of the full moon.

After the first few months she began to feel a change in herself. It became less and less easy for her to sit in the cold and dark and wait quietly for the raids to be over. She had to find devices to busy her thoughts. At first she studied Shakespeare's *Hamlet,* reading by the light of a candle stuck in a saucer. Next she turned to comparative religions; and ancient Chinese history, too, with its brief texts and elaborate commentaries, and also the writings of the golden age of Chinese poetry in the Tang Dynasty.

But as months began to turn into years the raids kept on and on. And now my friend would often find herself trembling from a new turbulence of thought. Her dreams turned into nightmares, visions of vengeance against the cities of the enemy, punishments more terrible than the fate of Sodom and Gomorrah. And she was beginning to find it harder to think straight and clear; she told herself she needed something that called for more concentration than the reading of classics.

There was living then, in the neighborhood, a young Belgian priest who had taken a Chinese name. My friend's background is wholly Protestant; but she revered the piety and good sense of this twenty-seven-year-old pastor who called himself Père Wei; a devout and consecrated man. One day she asked him if he would care to help her improve her French. While she could read his language, her pronunciation, she knew, was imperfect. So Father Wei began, during the raids, to coach her in pronunciation and also in grammatical rules. Deep in the caves, with hundreds crowded together, and the air foul and dark, they managed to carry on the lessons. He would start:

"The subjunctive mood denotes——"

Crash! Another bomb.

"—in general, what is viewed as——"

Smash! Another building destroyed.

"—being desirable——"

Boom! Clatter!

"—or undesirable——"

Bang!

At first the lessons were helpful. To concentrate on irregular verbs and syntax was a kind of temporary surcease, but the everlasting persistence of the raiding soon infuriated my troubled friend so that, however hard she tried, she could barely listen.

That was why, one April morning, she foolishly lingered too long out of doors. It was a day of bright sunshine, with the smell of wildflowers and new life spreading on the soft, spring breezes. They had just lived through another raid; the thought of going down into the caves again was suddenly intolerable.

"Father Wei," she said, "they won't be back for a little while longer, I'm sure! Let's sit here by this rattan table and study like human beings—*not like animals in the ground.*"

He gave her a mild glance, as if surprised by her tone, but he made no protest. As she sat down, a French lesson book in her hand, her body, mind, and soul were in turmoil. It was not going to be easy to concentrate, even in the spring air.

Suddenly she looked up and saw her husband standing at the entrance of the cave. He was beckoning her inside.

"Don't stay out there. You can never be sure," he called, and turned back. She could see him dimly as he descended the dark and narrow corridor that led into the cave. She should have answered his summons, but in that moment she furiously resented, not her husband's call, but the need for it. So she lingered.

Then almost instantly, as from nowhere, a distant drone, speeding toward them—enemy planes!

She sprang up, dropping her book and running toward the entrance, Father Wei close behind her. Then—chaos! There was a roar, a concussion, blackness. When her brain cleared, she was lying face down on the rough floor, cut and bruised, but just safely within the sheltering corridor. As she lay, in the dark, and yet with her mind miraculously clearer than in a long time, a voice seemed to speak to her. Was it her husband? Or the priest? It was neither: it was like a voice within herself.

"You have been saved from the Japs again. But what can save you from yourself?"

From herself? What did that mean? Her husband and the priest were lifting her, almost carrying her down the steep corridor.

Save her from herself? She was sitting in a chair. A doctor was examining her. But her thoughts were not on her body. There was a battle within.

"You were so near to death, only a few minutes ago," one part of her was saying. "You are alive now only because of the mercy of God. Must not you also be merciful?"

Yes, to all, to everyone—except, of course, the Japs.

"Even the Japs," the inner voice was telling her.

Forgive the Japs! The very thought seemed criminal, treason to the sacred cause. They had ravaged and pillaged, tortured and maimed, bayoneted babies and grandmothers, burned Chinese people alive, starved them to death . . .

It was unthinkable to forgive the Japs. Yet in the fluttering light of a few candles, a part of her was urging even that forgiveness.

"I curse the Japs!" she told herself stubbornly.

But the inner voice would not be silenced:

"Curses fall back on the curser. Hate destroys the hater!"

Through the gloom she could see Father Wei. Probably he was praying. And somehow she knew he would be praying for all the people of the world.

When the "all-clear" signals sounded, her husband walked with her to where the rattan table and chair had been—and were no more. A piece of shrapnel had cut the French grammar in half; its battered pages lay on the terrace. She still treasures the two pieces, for to her they are symbols of what almost happened to her in soul as well as in body. With the shattered book leaves in her hands, she understood at last the meaning of the question: What could save her from herself?

The Japs had not been able to destroy her, but by her hatred of them she had been destroying herself! The very hatred she had nursed was destroying her efficiency, her ability to fight on. She must fight, not like a dragon, but like the knightly St. George, who saved the people but did not become like the beast he slew. She could even ask God to open the eyes of the oppressors, to change them. Not curses but prayers were needed for the dream of victory and peace.

"Much has happened to my unhappy country, to my husband and to me, since that April morning in the bomb shelter," my friend told me. "But through it all—through defeat and illness I have been able to carry on with a sense of confidence and faith and inner peace.

"What came to me like a providential vision in the dug-out, now, in more peaceful surroundings, seems a kind of spiritual common sense. In great matters or small, hate is a painful and bitter experience. If we are wise, we will make haste to forgive, and get rid of the pain and bitterness before we get sick from them.

" *'And, throughout all eternity, I forgive you, you forgive me!'*

"That is the beginning of true freedom—when we are liberated from ourselves."

And I could see the peace in her eyes, more radiant than ever, as she paused, near the open door, before the photograph of a soldier in uniform. There were vases of red blossoms placed before the picture, and I knew it was the likeness of her husband. Then we shook hands and I took leave of my hostess, Madame Chiang Kai-shek.

15

THE NEW CRUSADE

*M*ADAME CHIANG, Mary Greenwillow, Rose Hawthorne, so many others—each gave to the God they knew and loved the service each could individually best perform. Famous or unknown, rich or poor, each lived out a life in honor of God.

One voice, echoed by others, can carry across a city. One spark, caught and held by others, can light a continent. One good Christian, joined with others, can change the lives of millions yet unborn.

The New Crusade is a proposal to individual Christians. It is not a suggestion for united mass action of any kind; I do not seek to form another pressure group. I appeal for personal action—one-man, one-woman crusades, a you crusade and a me crusade. The purpose is to find a way in which each of us can collaborate to help change the face of things as they are, and to help shape a better world in the things that are to come. Reform of mankind begins with you and me.

That proposition may sound fantastic, I realize, especially when one considers it in the light of the great needs of the time—and apparently, at least, far beyond the reach of any single person. Yet I am utterly serious in this proposal.

How can one little life operate so that it can help to prevent a third world war? Yet a third world war must be prevented, if the earth is to be safe for any one little life. How can any of us, the unelected and unappointed and unpolitical masses of the people, make our hopes and dreams so imperative upon our representatives that they will establish firmly a real and honest new international order of peace, justice, mercy, and security? That need for world organization looks back at us from the face of the map, wherever we turn.

But how can you or I make the lawmakers of the globe respect our insistence that atomic energy be controlled for constructive ends; that it be developed to bring not death but life? Today people everywhere live in a kind of leashed but constant panic; while they work, and in their dreams at night, fear is at their elbow. Again, how can we help to banish poverty and hunger from the world? What can one individual do to help put an end to the enslavement of other human beings, our brothers and sisters under God, enslaved by exploitation of greedy men, by forced labor and totalitarian tyranny?

Now let us turn our eyes nearer home. How can a God-fearing, goodhearted, ordinary, everyday man or woman help to increase good will and a square deal all around in the relations between labor and management? How help to combat the hatred and discrimination of race and religion? How can we help to break the log jam and get a real housing program under way? What can we do to so improve our own immediate society that crime, drunkenness, and moral looseness shall be halted and diminished?

What can we do to strengthen and make more wholesome family life?

I mention a few of the outstanding problems that confront us today; the frightening and yet challenging catalogue is by no means complete. The world is ill. Modern life has a sickness. But it is not one clear case of measles; it is what doctors who couldn't find what was wrong used to call a "complication of diseases." It is a complication of fear and its satellite hatreds; of greed, of hunger for power, of blood thirst, of ignorance, of indifference, incompetence and utter and complete despair—the last and worst virus of all, born in the unclean quagmire of abandoned faith, of lost hope, the soul trap of atheism.

Because a large part of mankind is already caught in that trap, because so many are stricken with that weird complication of diseases of the soul, every Christian is needed in the New Crusade. It is no longer possible to be a lazy Christian. This is the time for choosing sides, for showing of colors, for taking part. The enemy is very busy trying to cut Christianity into pieces, then to devour it at leisure. We can defeat his purpose. We can make the teachings of Christ victorious in the world. The only necessity is for Christians to be Christian. By this I mean the sacraments, union with Christ in the true Church, the power of grace and the way we live our private life.

It is true, and I know it, that the prospect looks dark. The forces of reaction, the scoffers at Christian principles and practice, gain new victories every day. For the sake of one atheist child, lapsed-time religious instruction is attacked in court. Everywhere the counsel of the ungodly is published as the modern, sensible way of life. The current wave of godlessness offers nothing but disillusion. It tears away everything sacred. It gives nothing in return. "Your coat is out of fashion!" it shouts to its victims, and tears off the cloak and throws it over the shoulder of the world. "Your food is not according to modern dietetics"—and it yanks bread from the hand. "Your house is out of date"— and it tears it down. Cold, hungry, shelterless—the newly emancipated man stands there, quite miserable in his emancipation.

Give him the warmth of the mantle of the Lord! Feed him the bread of life. Lead him to the altar. All this we may be able to do—if he recognizes the example our life can give for such as he. The poor victim is bare to the winds of life! In his unhappy state he yearns for help. But often he does not know where to turn. Your crusade is already started if your life offers opportunity to all who are seeking spiritual health, if in your own quiet devotion you can offer an example to those who are hungry for the water of everlasting life and find their own wells dry.

Live your own well! Live it with Christ at your side, as if He knew each thought and beheld each action, which, in truth, He does. You can join the crusade by renewing your faith, by rendering redoubled service, by more zeal.

What, specifically, can you do? You can begin by redoubling your prayers, not only night and morning, but all day long.

Live prayer unceasingly. That will open new gates for you, new opportunities will come to you, and new power to use them. The one eager to serve is quickly recognized.

We can also practice all the Christian virtues in our daily work. In the office, in the grocery market—wherever we are we are making an impression, good or bad, on other people. Because we are Christian, they will judge us as

Christians. Thus, whenever we are in contact with some other person, we can be a good or bad advertisement for our faith. That is the second step we can take in our own personal crusade; we can add to the fame of our faith by a smile when they know we have a right to be angry; by kindness and understanding and forgiveness. Through us the patience of Christ when His enemies spat upon Him can be shown again. His love, His forgiveness, His inspiration can flow through us. We can never foresee when and how our readiness to be the spigot through which the power of God can flow may bring to others the water of life.

Living for Christ is the most exciting adventure on which a human soul can embark. Each day, even each waking hour, is a challenge—as if we were wrestling with Evil itself. So—we smiled at the child who stamped his heel on our corns? Good enough. But wait, my friend. Here is a man who says I have a silly mind. He does, does he? . . . Easy does it, O my soul!

People *do* say such hurtful things, and it *is* so hard to forgive; but that is what makes the crusade exciting, the challenge an adventure. Because overcoming ourselves is the supreme test of strength and will power, and those who win are real champions for Christ.

The world needs a new crusade for Christianity, each Christian a crusader on his own. Furthermore, the crusade is needed internationally, nationally, locally, and in our private lives. And there, I urge upon you, is where the crusade must begin—in our own devoted lives. Back to devotion, back to our knees, and the crusade is already started. It is not weak because each of us seems to stand as one alone. We do not stand alone. We kneel before God and His power enters into us. We are like radium—small to the eye but possessed of undying force. By our private lives we should cast a glow, like radium of the soul, and light up the darkness for others, groping and frightened people.

Helping them is the beginning of our work. But there is more for us to do. Just as the active Christian has both duties and opportunities in his private life and in his home community, so he has a part to play on the national scene.

Every four years every American adult has, in the role of a United States national, the duty and the opportunity to cast his ballot for the next President of his country. But while presidential elections come only once every four years, a role in national affairs, however humble or obscure an active Christian may be, can be continuous, uninterrupted, and effective.

This statement means, to begin with, that we must be interested in national affairs and try to understand them. So again I remind you of the need to keep yourself informed.

It means knowing not only your city and state representatives, but also the names of your representatives in the upper and lower Houses. Those senators and representatives are your agents. Theoretically, at least, they are your servants. You pay their salaries. The money for their pay comes from the taxes which you pay. Certainly your wishes should concern them—and your objections, your indignation, your praise. If we write them frequently, they may feel inclined to consider us a nuisance, and say we bother them too much—but what will we Christians bother them about except the issues which threaten a Christian civilization? On such items we *ought* to bother them—morning, noon, and night!

If enough voters in their districts do bother them, they will take heed. For in their whimsical moments they will admit to you that the first duty of an officeholder is to be re-elected; otherwise he will no longer be an officeholder.

What are the aspects of national affairs of greatest concern to active Christians?

First, foremost, basic, is the need for simple, old-fashioned honesty in the thinking and acting of public officials. I do not mean merely to be on our guard against their misappropriation of our money. Theft is a crime that can be punished. I refer specifically to dishonesty of the intellect, by which some politicians whitewash a black thing and call it pure; the depravity of the sense of public obligation that makes some of them hide the truth, or distort it; goads them to offer false promises, when they know it is impossible to keep them, and all such cheapjack imposture born in the undemocratic conviction of some politicians that the people are fools.

There is an old Latin adage: *"Mundus vult decipi; ergo, decipiatur."* That means, roughly, "The world wishes to be deceived; therefore, let it be deceived." Once upon a time the quotation was the motto of jugglers and sleight-of-hand performers, roadside tricksters, pretenders to occult powers. But today it belongs more properly to a class of professional political deceivers who, in their own words, put it over on the public; tricksters pretending to be statesmen.

Today it is true, furthermore, that the world has had enough trickery in high places; it no longer wishes to be deceived; it demands the truth. That demand is a part of the Christian opportunity.

For such tricksters, living or dead, there should be no excuses. To deceive the voters, to betray the people may not be a crime, but it is a sin and as such is never to be condoned by the active Christian. He must add his strength to all other forces for good in standing for old-fashioned incorruptibility and those ancient, Christian ideals of personal honor which must again be the mark and sign of American statesmen.

So we must condemn, by voice and letter, all deceit practiced against us. We must make these servants of ours tell us the truth or we must get rid of them. We must make them keep their promises or we must fire them. We must insist that our servants return to the Christian code of morality, in thought and action, or else they must get out of public office. Nothing less than honor will do.

It is because the American people have been lenient and lackadaisical in the face of official intellectual corruption that they have so often been bamboozled and betrayed. We who voted such men into office have been remiss in our Christian duty, especially when we shrugged our shoulders and asked: "What else do you expect—in politics?" We must expect and demand a great deal more, and not resort to an easy, comfortable brush-off. For the third time I warn you that democracy is on trial, totalitarianism, with its atheism and power cruelty, is just around the corner—and there is no longer time or place in our world for a comfortable Christian.

We active Christians will be especially vigilant about attacks on religion. In all the courts today the atheists are busy sniping at the believers in God. Raising the cry of constitutional rights, they really want to destroy the mother of all rights, the freedom of religion. Some are sincere fanatics, hating God; still others are the agents of that Red Fascism which calls itself Communism.

We will keep ourselves well informed about all this, very busy in our New Crusade. In doing so we will remember that freedom of religion means freedom from molestation in the exercise of our religious freedom, and freedom from insult. We will view with suspicion the activities in the democratic process of men who traduce Christ's holy name and tell the Son of God to get out of the way to make room for Stalin. When national conferences are addressed by men who hold such sacrilegious views as that, we must be on the alert for the deliberations, resolutions, and recommendations of the leaders who sponsor such speakers. And we must make our revulsion felt to them—and to those who support them.

Let us, however, never breed hatred against those who hate us so palpably and viciously; let us defend our rights as good Christians and good citizens, with calmness and forgiveness—and the truth.

It is not an easy task to be a good citizen in a democracy. The job calls for a study of issues and of men, for alertness in national affairs, for Christian charity in the face of active and skilled anti-religious activities, and for even more Christian charity and forbearance toward the enemies of our way of life. Yet it is precisely in that charity that we have victory over evil. To fail in that is to put overpowering weapons in the hands of enemies. For, "Look," they will cry, "these hypocritical people are just as bad as we are. They pretend to renounce hate, and yet see how they hate us."

We must not hand them such a triumph. Instead, we shall illustrate our principles by applying them in every encounter.

In this broad spirit of Christian sympathy we must, nevertheless, be active in opposition to all moves, all schemes to bring about the tyranny of Red totalitarianism, or any other form of tyranny. We must give our strength to protest movements against the furtherance of totalitarianism, Fascist or Communist, anywhere in this land, whether in the halls of Congress, the bureaucracy of administrative government, or in the offices of lobbyists. Ours can never be, except accidentally, the view of one party against another; ours is a pure Christian point of view, needed no matter what group is in power. In this cause we write letters and telegrams, sign petitions and let our views be known.

In this same broad spirit we work to press home, in a time of indifferentism and selfish preoccupation, the virtues of the Christian life—the teaching Church and the reality of the Christian experience. Here there is a real hope, a real chance for our free way of life to endure; otherwise it is bound to perish. That is because the Christian way of life is founded on the divine revelation of what is sound and just and true. At our peril we turn our backs on the instruction, for the law is fixed and the results are certain. So far as the outcome is concerned, belief or disbelief is of no consequence. You are free to reject the law of gravity if you wish. You can denounce it as a great superstition, keeping human reason in bondage. But you violate it at your peril. Don't step off the roof!

The moral laws are equally fixed. You may laugh at the injunction against divorce, but you cannot laugh off the rising tide of juvenile delinquency, the result of broken homes.

It is our opportunity to remind the officeholders of the moral law and let them know it is important to us. The hope of the world is that Christians shall be filled with consuming zeal and press home at every vital point in our national affairs the Christian point of view.

I urge you all to be active in the New Crusade—not to see things under the bed, of course, but not to be taken in by the forces of Evil which today are fighting a life-and-death battle to take our religious freedom from us—in the name of democracy.

16

THE FUTURE IS OURS

WHEN the United Nations was founded in the great parliament of peoples at San Francisco, there was no mention of Almighty God.

Men, met to plan for peace on earth, ignored the source of all peace. The founders of the new world society behaved exactly as if there were no such source—as if men, by themselves, could bring to earth the kingdom of Heaven. They behaved as if they were a congress of atheists!

Yet they were, of course, nothing of the kind. In the great gathering there were many pious men—a majority—in whose hearts lay the love and fear of God.

Why, then, did they fail to mention Him?

They did so in deference to the one officially atheistic power represented there. One God-denying nation was able to overrule fifty other nations, including the United States, on whose silver coins appears the legend "In God We Trust." Nothing that has happened in recent years more explicitly illustrates the need for religious influence in world affairs.

Let us, as Christians, look at the world. We look at it

in a time unique in its history; unique because its population is not any longer made up of a series of isolated groups. Whether we like it or not, it *is* one world—except as men divide it up again—not in space but in ideas. And if civilization is to survive, it must become a much better world than it is today as we look at it, teetering drunkenly on the edge of another war.

In whatever direction we look this danger is apparent. In China greed and the lust for power still contend against those who would have peace. Palestine is a powder keg and the fuse is lit. We are already in a cold war and the temperature is rising. How preposterous all this seems! Only a little while ago we talked so learnedly of the four freedoms and of the eight points of President Roosevelt and Winston Churchill. Ask the first man on the street to name you those eight points. No, ask yourself. Never mind!

All during the dreadful years of conflict against Fascism and Nazism, we talked of the highest ideals of freedom. But when the fighting stopped and the peacemakers *got* together, they found that they could not *stay* together. Since then there has been a constant division among the victor nations. It is a most pertinent fact that the nation which refused to let God into San Francisco is the same nation that will not let peace into Europe.

Let us not mince words. Godless Russia has obstructed peace. Atheistic Communism has kept the world in foment ever since the war came to a halt.

You will hear a great many students of our foreign policy say that the basic mistake made by the United States and England was in appeasing Russia—giving in to her, bending over backward to be co-operative. I believe our leaders should have had the common sense to realize that these appeasements were bound to fail because the differences between the countries are fundamental.

The Communist nations believe that man is no more than a speck of dust. He has no soul, no future life, and no God to whom he is responsible. He is, therefore, responsible only to the State. So the Communists set up a dictatorship and govern man as a trained animal is governed by a circus performer.

The free nations believe that an individual is the unit, the most important unit of value in a community—and that he must be treated as such. They look upon a person as a child of God with an immortal destiny. This concept is held not only by Christians but by other sects represented in the United Nations. The Buddhists, the Moslems, and many others, however darkly misinformed as to the true faith, are nevertheless worshipers of an Almighty God. So they, too, have respect for the individual.

This basic difference in concept, in outlook, is far more important than political disagreements. Indeed, the political differences spring from this basic difference. That fact should have been recognized at San Francisco, and appeasement should have stopped there. The mass of public opinion, represented by an overwhelming majority of the member states, should have prevailed. Russia should have been told that while she was not obligated to join in worship to God she must, as a minority of one, respect the deepest feelings of the majority. Instead, by one single vote she vetoed God. She made all the others behave as if they, too, were atheists—which they were not. That might seem to be water over the dam now—but it is not.

The Christian forces of America and England and France and other countries can still make themselves heard by constant agitation on this principal and basic matter. It is only necessary that good citizens take an interest in the United Nations and insist that the moral law govern its deeds. Until the common man does make his influence felt in these high deliberations, the United Nations will continue to be the feckless and ineffective spectacle that it has continued to be since it began.

Only God can help the United Nations today!

Its spiritual power has been sterilized by atheistic objection, but even now that power can be brought into its deliberations with such redemptive force that the new world organization can take on life for the first time, strength for the first time.

If the Russians protest that their atheism is insulted by prayer at the sessions of the United Nations, we can say that our Christianity has already been deeply insulted by its absence.

Now it may well be asked: What can a lone Christian do against the isolation and intellectual splendor of that august assemblage?

The answer is that every Christian has a pipe line to infinite power by his own prayers. We can pray, every one of us, for a change of attitude in this attempt at world peace. We can urge others to do so. More than that, we can urge the delegates themselves to pray. And we can, by writing our representatives, in hundreds and thousands and hundreds of thousands of letters, plead with them to demand in open council that the help of God be asked to inspire these agents of democracy, these legislators of world affairs with wisdom to accomplish a real triumph.

The skeptic will grin at this. He will say that brains and not prayers are needed. The answer to that is that the brains have had their chance and have made a sorry mess. All through history brains have tried to make a world government. If you depended on brains, you would have to remember that one attempt after another in history to establish world friendliness turned out to be no more than a fantastic dream. The idea of a world alliance is not new. Since the time of the ancient Greeks it has been proposed and tried—and it has always failed.

The Italian poet Dante called for a world empire in his *De Monarchia*—unity and arbitration to end maddening chaos. Then there was the "Grand Design" of Henri Quatre. Hugo Grotius in 1625 wrote his great book suggesting a code of international law. William Penn wanted a supreme parliament of nations. Czar Alexander I of Russia founded the Holy Alliance after the Napoleonic Wars.

None of them worked!

Yet on the North American continent we saw a group of little states, each of which might have become a kingdom like a European monarchy, but all of which united to form one nation, the United States of America—a land where the freedom of men transcends any freedom in history. Today that same country is the strongest in the world. Where lay the difference? How did our experiment succeed where all others failed?

You may find the answers in the Declaration of Independence and in the Constitution of our country. There it is plainly stated that the freedoms of our individuals are bestowed not by a state, nor by a government, but are natural rights that belong to each one of us because each one of us is a child of Almighty God.

The free and successful alliance of the American states

was born in a climate of faith. There were prayers at the Constitutional Convention. It is a matter of opinion, but in spite of all that has been said, I do not believe that there was a single atheist among the delegates, although there may have been some agnostics. If there were atheists there, they were a minority, as is Russia a minority today in the world assembly, and their atheistic views did not override the religious convictions of the majority.

If there were atheists at the Constitutional Convention, they were not appeased!

This country's birth certificate, the Declaration, time and again pays tribute to the Heavenly Father and looks to Him for help. Our national baptism was in blood, and the certificate of the baptism was our Constitution, with all its reverence for the dignity of man as a child of God.

Why is the world so blind to the immense significance of this difference? We began with God's help, and with God's help we are still here.

What are the dangers to us now at home and abroad? Do they come from the believers in the God who has been so good to us? Ah, no. They come from the disciples of Karl Marx, whose views on religion, whose hatred of God were later to be echoed by each new aspirant to world mastery, including Mussolini and Hitler and now Stalin. Is it not clear, this significance?

Is it not plain that we must go back to the God of our youth; that the United Nations must become His instrument if we are to have peace? For that we must pray; for that we must ask others to pray; for that we must ask our delegates to have the courage required to make prayer a part of the proceedings. Here is a chance for the Christian to play his part on the international scene. If that is done, if the piety of the delegates at Philadelphia, of Washington at Valley Forge, and of Lincoln after the second battle of Bull Run is imitated at Lake Success, then the climate of our dangerous time will change and the dream of peace will come closer to us all.

God grant that this may be! But as yet it is only one of the three possibilities for the future. There is also a chance that we may find ourselves suddenly at war. And there is the third possibility that we may fall back into the old uneasy scheme of armament races and power politics. Let no man tell us he knows which of these three possibilities is most likely. To us the future remains the same dark mystery it was for all the generations before us, a constant riddle of hope and danger.

We shall be better off if we refuse to be elated by the wishful fantasies of dreamers or be cast down by the nightmares of dejected *soi-disant* realists. Our serenity must lie in the fact that it matters little what the future holds for us of good or evil; it matters greatly how we shall meet our fortune.

In this truth there is, for every one of us, the hope of good life. It means that we can decide for ourselves the issue of our happiness or despair. That is a great Christian privilege. The attitude is everything!

We are, so psychologists tell us, the sum total of our attitudes; their compound is our personality. But this knowledge of the psychologists is belated; by laboratory methods they have merely rediscovered the ancient scripture which taught us: "As a man thinketh in his heart, so is he." Here is the secret of the only true security.

Our task on the road before us, individually and nationally, is to preserve the attitudes that gave life and growth to Christian civilization.

It is easy to fall into the wrong attitudes. One citizen says: "Democracy means that I am as good as you are." That represents his attitude. It is an aggressive, chip-on-the-shoulder point of view that sooner or later will have to be defended by force. Another man says: "Democracy means that you are as good as I am." That is an altogether different attitude, one that will never need to be defended, in good times or bad.

I am reminded of an American soldier who woke upon the operating table of a field hospital behind the lines of the battle of the Bulge. The surgeon smiled down with tender encouragement and said:

"Son, you're going to be all right! I'm only sorry that I have to tell you one piece of bad news—you lost your arm!"

The soldier grinned back and muttered:

"I didn't lose it—I gave it!"

The point of view of that maimed soldier will influence all his future years. Misfortune has no weapon to break the spirit of a good man.

It is still hard for us to believe that misfortune can be a friend in disguise; easy to forget that obstacles in our path are actually and literally our greatest opportunities. Demosthenes became a great orator, not in spite of but because of his stammering. Sir Walter Scott, whose greatness as poet and novelist has not yet been dimmed altogether by his detractors, owed his fame to a misfortune of a peculiarly unjust kind. As you may well remember, he wrote his novels, sacrificing his health to pay back money he had never received—debts contracted by foolish business partners. Scott could have followed a popular modern custom and put his firm through bankruptcy. Instead, he decided to earn the money himself and pay off debts of half a million. He already had a double job, as deputy sheriff in Selkirkshire and clerk of the court; nevertheless, he wrote his famous story, *Waverley,* in four weeks; nine major books followed in three years. To cancel bankruptcy he wrote a total of forty-eight volumes. Why did he do this? He did it because he was a man of principle; because he believed in certain ideals of honor, he rejected the easy course of expediency. In the process he gave to the world a treasure-store of romance.

Of course when Sir Walter left school he did not expect any future like that. Today's June graduates have an advantage there: uncertainties confront them in the very vestibule of life. It is bound to be a bewildering experience —to open the door into a world that seems immediately bent on destroying itself; to look down the four winds and see everywhere only confusion and chaos. And it is natural to complain to oneself:

"Why was I not born in some easygoing, old-fashioned time when everything was peaceful and a fellow could get a job, propose to his girl friend, and plan out a life?"

Let us hope our young people will do all those things with great success. But let us not deceive ourselves; there never was a time when everything was peaceful; not since Eden have human beings really had an easygoing period; the enchantment of other days is lent by distance. That is not to deny, however, that these are unusually turbulent days. They are, indeed, most sorry and uncertain—and perhaps these are signs of their greatness and significance.

I can imagine a young man on a New Jersey farm many years ago wishing that he had lived when calm lay over the thirteen colonies and there was no ragged army calling him away from the plow and the neighbor's daughter to march where George Washington told him to march.

The glory of such marches was not visible in the youth of the reluctant farmer. Even the meaning of the struggle was obscured. Not until years afterward would men realize that the colonial troops had fought not merely to throw off the odious authority of absentee government. What they really achieved in their victory was such liberty as men had nowhere before enjoyed.

I am perfectly sure, too, that there were boys and girls in the pioneer families all the way to the Pacific Coast who wondered why they could not have been born in the comfort and gaiety of seaboard towns, where forests, wild beasts, and Indians no longer got in the way of progress.

These young men of olden times, if they could speak to us today, might not be willing to concede that our future is more threatening than was theirs. I suspect they would also point out to us our superior advantages. To them the smallest comforts of our daily lives would seem Arabian-night luxuries. They did not possess the wisdom of the ages to which we have been exposed in our schools. What would they have thought if they had been told they were actors in an historic drama, indispensable players in the advancing pageant of civilization? Yet that is what they were.

We cannot see our little lives in perspective, but we can believe there is a perspective. Perhaps we may not grasp even the nature of the historical process, or the character of the result, but we can hold onto our faith in the destiny of our people and, in good conscience, help it along a little.

Daily throughout our lives let us renew our faith in

Christian attitudes—and keep our sense of humor while we are about it.

So it has been from our beginning. Let us never forget that this country was founded in a climate of faith and good spirits by men who recognized the limitations of mortal thought and relied upon the inspiration of Almighty God—and who had the capacity for laughter. In their darkest seasons they smiled at each other and said: "We must all hang together or we shall certainly hang separately." Such men did not need the discoveries of modern scientists to instruct them that there were limits to man's intellectual capacity. They had the humility to know that for themselves in 1776. Because the complexities of their problems seemed beyond their powers to resolve, they laughed at their own plight and prayed for help from above. The great documents of our Revolution were composed under the benediction of laughter and prayer.

Surely this unique faith was justified! Surely there was more than mere human ingenuity, something touched with the divine in the great triangular division of the new government's powers: the legislative, judicial, and executive trinity. The workability of the new mechanism was matched by its elastic adaptability to changing conditions. The Constitution grew with the country, because its genius was a living thing with the power to expand and develop. Never yet has its character changed nor its attitudes been altered. Now, as in the beginning, it is the charter of free men.

In launching that charter the founding fathers knew that their experiment invited disaster. Since they believed the inspiration to make men free with such unparalleled liberties came from God, they believed also that only with

His help could it prosper. That was why they wrote the words in silver—"In God We Trust." On our money they stamped their prayer. Their faith is our inheritance and our trust. May we never lose it!

After World War I men in Europe did lose all faith in such freedom. Because of doubt and discouragement they allowed tyrants to fasten chains on their souls. In the confusion and chaos of that unsettled time they welcomed the strong man who promised to make everything run on time. No longer trusting in God, themselves, or the system of their government, the frightened people exalted their dictators and collaborated in the degradation of their own dignity.

No one can deny that the dictators exhibited a certain superficial efficiency. They did manage to get things done. And why not? Democracy will always be maddeningly slow; it takes time to persuade and convince those who disagree with you; it is much quicker for the despot to imprison or kill his opponent. The efficiency of totalitarianism, so far as it goes, is invariably a product of immorality —wickedness on a grand scale, made possible because frightened peoples relinquish the moral authority of the ballot and of free institutions to seek shelter in the brutal rule of force.

Our pessimists are not entirely unreasonable when they suggest that we ourselves may follow the examples of Italy, Germany, and Russia. If we become sufficiently frightened, that tragic blunder is possible. We may tear up the Declaration of Independence, the Constitution and its amendments; we may tear down the statues of Washington and Lincoln and begin to salute a shiny new dictator, God forbid!

I believe that God *will* forbid it. We have not lost our American heritage, although in recent years we have seemed to neglect it. I can look back to the end of World War I, which ushered in what has been called "the debunking period." For a while that project in disillusion was a needed and tonic experience. But having cast off the shackles of stuffiness, we were not satisfied but proceeded to trample on good taste as well—and finally on good sense. "All things must be laid low" seemed to be the cry of the iconoclasts. Our heroes were besmirched as hypocrites, frauds, and fools. Our morals were mocked at, our standards lowered, in a carnival of repudiation that was like a *Walpurgisnacht*. And all this cynicism was offered as if it were itself a brave new faith, a kind of new nobility that appealed to our liberalism and our fortitude!

Yet if those who were dethroned had oversentimentalized the facts of life for us, the newcomers brutalized the same facts until they were false indeed.

It is the thrilling opportunity of the new generation to join in that rebuilding; to cherish the old faith in the midst of new perils; and, scorning fear, to face the world with attitudes born of principle rather than expediency.

There you have the heart of today's battle—principle versus expediency, a new phase of a very old struggle indeed.

He who holds to principle is prepared to lose advantage for the sake of something more precious than life, even. He who practices expediency will give up no advantage, sacrifice nothing; he wants what he wants when he wants it, and he will take it by unrestrained action.

In private life the one is called a social person, the

other an antisocial person. The terms apply to nations and to governments as well.

Here we see the moral choice humanity must make between the immense contradiction of two attitudes. The time is coming when we must decide what we believe. Is it better to give than to receive? Or should we get what we can, while we can? It is idle to evade the issue; that is democracy against totalitarianism, Christianity against Communism, good against evil.

Many Christian men and women have been tricked into believing that the social objectives of the Soviet ideology and of our Christian revelation are the same. Once again we hear the familiar and deceiving affirmation that there is a brave new faith, a courageous modern and more practical sort of nobility. "We want the best for all mankind," the Communists argue. "In our system all men are made truly equal. We have no rich, no poor. All are on the same level."

They fail to mention a savage difference. Communism seeks to drag all men down to the same level of enslavement by hate. Christianity seeks to lift all men up to a higher level of freedom through love. Between those two concepts lies an abyss deep as perdition itself. The difference is one of attitude.

Meanwhile, we know what things are good and what things are evil, and we shall give our devotion to the good attitude. So shall we stand with Almighty God. And if He is with us, who can be against us?

Other Challenging and Practical Books of
Faith and Inspiration
That You Will Want to Read and Reread by

FULTON OURSLER

THE GREATEST STORY EVER TOLD

Written in beautiful, simple language, THE GREAT-
EST STORY EVER TOLD paints a powerful and compel-
ling portrait of the greatest life ever lived, illuminated with
deep personal devotion and mature understanding and scholarship. The episodes in this reverently written, faithfully presented picture of the life of Christ are taken from the four
gospels. It recounts fully and exactly what happened during
the thirty-three years of the life of Jesus as recorded by the
apostles, Matthew, Mark, Luke, and John.

Also available in—

Handsome illustrated edition in a beautiful oversized for-
mat with sixteen pages of magnificent full-color paintings
by Kenneth Riley.

MODERN PARABLES

Fulton Oursler's modern parables are gems of the story-
teller's art. In six hundred to eight hundred words he tells a
tale from real life in the modern world—each an interesting,
dramatic, exhilarating story, and each an example of the power
of faith and religion in daily, simple living. These parables
have appeared in Mr. Oursler's weekly syndicated column and
have evoked such an enthusiastic response that this book is
the result. Sidney Fields, writing of the parables in his column
in the New York *Mirror,* had this to say:

"The first essentials in the art of storytelling are a sharp eye and a sharper ear. Fulton Oursler possesses both, and to them adds a magnificent simplicity and penetrating understanding that are fed by his deep faith. . . ."

FATHER FLANAGAN OF BOYS TOWN
(with Will Oursler)

Now for the first time the whole story of Boys Town, the man who created and guided it, and the real stories of the boys it served, is warmly and faithfully told. Boys Town is the monument, the tribute to a man who believed there were no bad boys, who believed any boy could be saved for himself and the community if given the proper understanding, training, food, shelter, security, and love. FATHER FLANAGAN OF BOYS TOWN is no mere story of brick and dollars; it is a story of a life and devotion that is unparalleled. It is a story with humor and kindliness, humanly told. "The deeply interesting life of a man who had a vision and lived up to it." —*Eleanor Roosevelt.*